MASTERING THE ART OF TEAM COACHING

A comprehensive guide to unleashing the power, purpose and potential in any team

GEORGINA WOUDSTRA

Mastering the Art of Team Coaching

A comprehensive guide to unleashing the power, purpose and potential in any team.

ISBN 978-1-838467-60-9

eISBN 978-1-838467-61-6

First published in 2021 and reprinted in 2023 by Team Coaching Studio Press

© Georgina Woudstra 2021

Team Coaching Wheel diagram © TCS

Printed in the UK

CONTENTS

ACKNOWLEDGEMENTS

Standing on the shoulders of giants

This book has been many years in gestation, so it is impossible to thank everyone who has contributed to and shaped my life and work. Writing doesn't come easily to me, which is partly why it took me so long. I am a practitioner at heart rather than an author, and like many who have dedicated themselves to their art, true learning happens in the arena in which they practise. In order for this tacit experience – unwritten and unexamined – to gradually turn into knowledge which could be refined and shared, I needed to understand what I was doing and why, and what worked and what didn't.

Along the way, I have been blessed to have had many teachers and colleagues who have assisted me in the process of making sense of my experiences in the arena and refining them into an approach that works. I would have been unable to succeed without them and I am eternally grateful. Thanks to my many guides, especially Sally Denham-Vaughan, Marie-Anne Chidiac, Rosemary Napper, Trudi Newton, Christine Thornton, Dorothy Siminovitch, Ruth Wageman, Krister Lowe and many others.

The approach described in this book is also the legacy of coaching forefathers Thomas Leonard, Sir John Whitmore and Laura Whitworth, all of whom enlightened me around coaching as a catalyst to unlock a person's potential. Coaching is never more vital than today, yet we need to go beyond the individual and unlock potential at group, team, organisational and societal levels. Also, gratitude to my friend Katherine Tulpa, global CEO of the Association for Coaching, for writing the foreword to this book. She is a leading light in coaching and has worked tirelessly for 20 years to give professional credence to our work.

The creation of the Team Coaching Studio (TCS) and the ideas that are encapsulated in this book are also fine examples of teamwork. I am deeply appreciative of everyone who has been part of the journey. Thank you, Annie Bennett, Bob Shearer, Sebastian Fox and Carroll Macey for your belief, support and courage to jump into the deep end. I am indebted to Declan Woods, a fellow pioneer who joined TCS in our infancy with equal dedication to mastery and shaping the field of team coaching. He has stood by me through thick and thin. And also deep gratitude to Allard de Jong, an immensely talented trainer, inspiring thinker and writer, collaborator and genuine friend. He ensures that I never have to think alone and helps me to translate complex ideas into a useable and practical form. He also makes me laugh – a lot – and that's more valuable than gold.

I also want to acknowledge the growing community of people around the world who are committed to evolving the field of team coaching. Over the next decade, their contribution will be far more significant than this book. I am greatly encouraged to see so many join us in this movement.

Also, Sue Richardson from The Right Book Company who has held my hand through this whole process, Simon Rae who cajoled me into storytelling and Chloe Robertson for her wonderful illustrations.

Pamela, my mother, bestowed on me a belief that you can achieve anything you set your mind on – this has been one of the most significant gifts in my life. My father, Laurence, gave me a warm heart and love of humour. My sister Sara, who abundantly provides love and support to our family and everyone she knows. I give deep gratitude to my daughter, Jasmine, who is quite the most beautiful soul I have ever known. Your capacity to think philosophically and to live according to your values is a lesson for us all.

And to my husband, Dan, who encourages me to follow my heart and to do what is mine to do. He provides unswerving help and steadfast support. He is my rock and, without him, this book would not exist.

Finally, thank YOU for generously giving your time and attention to my work. I dearly hope it serves you well.

FOREWORD

By Katherine Tulpa

> There can be no growth if we do not remain open and vulnerable to what is new and different.
>
> – JOHN O'DONOHUE, *To Bless the Space Between Us*

As one executive, a CEO leading a purpose-driven, multi-billion global asset management firm revealed to me: 'I'm now at a stage where I'm in pursuit of a coach who is more of an artist than a scientist.' Who, after working with five coaches throughout his career, was looking for deeper meaning in his life – or in his terms, more 'soul' – to enable future businesses and generations to evolve, and go beyond.

Likewise, there was a great pride and belief he evoked when describing his leadership teams. Recognising that in order for them go on this journey alongside him, they would each need to paint their own canvas, so that collectively they are creating a mosaic that inspires others to flourish and grow – with their own sense-making and 'right action' – for others to then exceed those before. Especially in our times of much-needed renewal.

In the Association for Coaching (AC), we often refer to this as the 'ripples' that coaches, in all their forms – e.g. executive coaches, team coaches, internal coaches and the leader or emerging 'leader coach' – create by applying a coaching mindset or approach in their interactions with others. It's been about the knowledge and practice of coaching, in our own pursuit as a profession to learn the ingredients for what makes an excellent coach.

We're also at a stage where escalating global challenges are accelerating the need for, and value of, coaching. For some it's manifesting – using the words of wisdom from the forefather Sir

John Whitmore – in 'a crisis of meaning'. In the 19 years since the AC has been established as a professional body – and in my own practice as a C-level executive and team coach – the work we do has never been so purposeful.

Added to this, companies large through small look to stay afloat during this uncertainty, at epic proportions. It's requiring leaders and especially teams to pull together, align on a vision, and collaborate as never before. Agile and remote working is the new norm in many organisational systems and structures that are now outdated, still mainly predominated by rational thought (e.g. the science) or what can be seen.

We're now in need of a 'refresh', as organisations experience their own crises of meaning at a system level. This paves the way for greater co-creation, connection and care (hence *the art*), to make a greater impact within their businesses and cultures.

For coaching – and especially team coaching – this is an invitation to evaluate and 'go beyond' the knowledge and practice of coaching, in our ongoing pursuit of excellence and mastery. To be vulnerable and open to the art of coaching, trusting what can't be seen.

This is where this very special and relevant book, *Mastering the Art of Team Coaching* is here to guide us. Truly, Georgina has made a significant contribution to our profession, most generously shared within these pages. This comes at a time within our profession when the demand for effective team coaching is on the rise, requiring coaches to be well equipped to deal with all its complexities, and be our best.

Having known Georgina for over two decades, as a friend, colleague, co-author and a speaker at AC conferences and masterclasses, no one is better equipped to write this book, in the authentic form it takes. Her pursuit to expand our awareness in working with teams in a holistic sense and instil a greater sense of inner calm and self-efficacy is evident.

She role models what's been elegantly captured in the teachings here, through years of study and applying her 'art' with teams in practice. Inherent within her approach is her passion for expanding the body of knowledge, practice and now art of team coaching.

Appropriately, *Mastering the Art of Team Coaching* also comes at a time when the AC is launching its new Team Coaching Accreditation scheme. So this book will provide a valuable resource for those demonstrating and enhancing their focus in this area.

In summary, I know I speak for so many colleagues throughout the world in saying how very grateful we are to Georgina for bringing her wisdom, in-depth knowledge and experience of working with teams to fruition. It's now up to us to expand upon on these teachings, to enrich or paint our own canvas, like any good master passes on to others.

This, in turn, will enhance the collective contributions we make to enable teams to innovate, be vulnerable and ride through the next waves of changes in front of them. To create a trusted space, where each person's voice is harnessed for the team to fully co-create and flourish. Enjoy!

Katherine Tulpa

Group CEO & co-founder, Association for Coaching,

February 2021

INTRODUCTION

Historically, pandemics have forced humans to break with the past and imagine their world anew. This one is no different. It is a portal, a gateway between one world and the next.

– ARUNDHATI ROY, 'The pandemic is a portal',
  Financial Times

Every human on this planet felt the impact of Covid-19 because of the immediate effects it had on daily living. We are, however, beset by far greater threats which predate the pandemic and which, if not addressed, will lead to irreversible and catastrophic devastation. We need to cross the abyss from a history marred by greed, destruction and fragmentation to a sustainable future inspired by collective and planetary wellbeing.

Otto Scharmer (2018) speaks of three major divides. The *ecological divide* of an economy that consumes the resources of 1.5 planets, resulting in environmental destruction and the loss of nature. The *social divide* where a handful of billionaires own as much as half of the rest of mankind. The *spiritual divide* compelling more than 800,000 people to commit suicide each year. He says, 'In essence, we are collectively creating results that (almost) nobody wants. These results include the loss of nature, the loss of society and the loss of Self.'

The challenge is so extraordinary, it requires a new approach to leadership and problem-solving. While some inspired political leadership is desperately needed, we are far beyond the point where any one individual, or set of individuals, however dynamic, focused and charismatic, can turn the tide. The problems are simply too extensive and too complex to be solved by the old models of top-down authority.

Collaboration is the key to resolving the challenges ahead at every level, from the global to the local. It will also be critical to the success of tomorrow's organisations, all of which will need to be orientated towards helping to clear up the mess we have made.

Of course, there are cynics who will prioritise short-term gain whatever the long-term cost; there are those who will deny the evidence even as the polar regions continue to melt and the sea levels continue to rise; and yet others who will passively accept the encroaching devastation with a shrug of despair. Pessimism is easy, even a bleak comfort. Instead, let us be guided by the words of Maya Angelou, who says 'Hope and fear cannot occupy the same space. Invite one to stay.'

Hope is our only chance, our guide and our inspiration. It must drive our development of a new, revolutionary way of doing things together. But this is not an easy option. Collaboration is as difficult, complex and challenging as it is vital.

The recognition of this truth has been increasing in the sphere of business coaching for a number of years. As one of the doyens in the field, Peter Hawkins (2011), strikingly puts it: 'The current world challenges task us as a species to find a way of working together, across disciplines and borders, beyond local and self-interest in a way that has never been attained before. In working together we need to generate new ways of thinking, for, as Einstein so memorably pointed out, you cannot solve a problem with the same thinking that created it.'

And in order to prosper, we will need to embrace the new story and the new lens for understanding the world and to develop a new mindset of working for the collective good rather than company gain or market dominance. It is a story of 'we' rather than 'I', and it calls on us to recognise that everything is interconnected – the world's problems and their solutions.

To survive – and thrive – companies will hire from a global marketplace; they will grow diverse, virtual workforces, take a cross-sector focus and construct shorter and more flexible projects and deals. Those that flourish will be motivated by a purpose so compelling that it will attract the best talent from around the world. These new ecosystems will be adaptable and flexible, with the capacity to respond confidently and quickly to emerging demands and challenges.

Such a radical change is not easy, but there are already many thousands of trained professionals to help with this vital transition. Team coaching has itself evolved out of one-to-one coaching as the need to derive the maximum from the talent pool in every firm has driven the emphasis from the individual to the team.

I believe we need to increase the number of team coaches, partnering with teams and networks of teams in order to unleash their potential to collaborate more effectively. And it is in the hope of contributing to this massively important process that I have written this book. In 2017 I founded Team Coaching Studio (TCS), an organisation dedicated to the development of team coaches around the world, consistently improving how teams work and collaborate. Our core beliefs at TCS are that teams are creative and resourceful. At their best they are the crucible of innovation, problem-solving and development.

However, time and again teams fall short of their potential. One of the problems is that many of today's leaders are the products of the culture of individualism, in which personal success (as defined by multi-million-pound salaries and a place in the *Sunday Times* Rich List) is the ultimate goal. This cult of the business superstar has long sustained the pyramid model of leadership in which policy decisions are taken by the few and then cascaded down to a subservient workforce below.

This model is now obsolete and must be replaced by collaboration and teamwork. The good news is that the skills required are identifiable and can be developed. Team coaches guide and challenge teams to work more effectively together, both within their own team and with other teams across alliances and partnerships.

But a note of caution. Team coaching is not for the faint hearted. Working with a team during an awayday to shape a new vision or craft their strategy can take skilful facilitation. But penetrating the surface of team dynamics, politics, power – the barriers to successful collaboration – takes real team coaching. Team coaching is challenging and unpredictable and you can't control the outcome.

It can take you to the edge of your capacity, to the limits of your courage and into the depths of your vulnerability. To be a great team coach requires that you work on yourself and your capacity to create a strong enough container for the work, to sit in the fire when the heat rises and to use yourself as an instrument of awareness, choice and change; this is where the magic lies. As Bill O'Brien, former CEO of Hanover Insurance, says, 'The success of an intervention depends on the interior condition of the intervener.' (Quoted in Scharmer 2018)

Team coaching is about creating spaces where teams can connect, think and rewire how they work together. It is not something you do to a team; it is something you do with a team. You must develop the approach within yourself, and model it for others, to be effective in applying it to teams.

Becoming a successful team coach is a long and arduous journey in which you will undoubtedly be tested. It takes time, humility, self-knowledge, self-compassion – and many hours of study and practice. Over time you will develop the skills and resilience to transform how people come together and collaborate to achieve an outcome that is greater than any individual could manage.

This work is vitally important and we are all part of a movement that has the capacity to help navigate through the troubles and challenges that confront us. You don't have to do it all alone. Join us and become part of a global community working to bring about collaboration for change around the planet.

Writing a book about team coaching is in some ways a contradiction in terms; after all, books are meant to be authoritative and, as the author, I am meant to have answers. This can lead you to hasten to extract the 'how to' from these pages. Team coaching doesn't work in this way. It is a lived experience between people and often takes those involved to places they could not have imagined before starting. My aim in this book is to offer a road map, without being overly prescriptive, to help you find your own way.

I will begin by setting the context for 'the work'. The world around us is ever changing, placing new demands on leaders and teams. The circumstance that we find ourselves in needs to frame and shape our approach to team coaching, so no two commissions should ever be the same. If you find yourself wheeling out a cookie-cutter approach to team coaching, then you may be forgetting the uniqueness of each situation.

The remainder of the book is dedicated to the complex role of the team coach. In addition to disseminating the methodology and philosophy of team coaching as practised by all of us at TCS, I have decided to share extensively my own personal experiences to illustrate the many challenges that you could encounter (please note that these stories are composites of real experiences, to preserve client confidentiality). My hope is that this frank exploration of highs and lows from my own experience will prove stimulating and reassuring. No one gets everything right all the time, but if we learn from mistakes – our own or other people's – we will be better practitioners and of more value to our clients. And to see how a difficult situation can be turned around and transformed into a resounding success should generate the self-confidence to do likewise.

At the end of each chapter, you are invited by Dr Declan Woods to engage in 'reflection time'. If your intent is to speed read through in order to get to the next book in the pile by your desk, then you might be tempted to skip this section. However, if you are on a quest for mastery in team coaching then I encourage you not to bypass this leg of your journey, as your effectiveness as a team coach is directly related to your capacity to step back, reflect and to think for yourself. And, if you have not yet found a reflective practice that works for you, then I recommend Declan's article on 'Coaches' Use of Reflective Journals for Learning' (Woods, 2011).

 A bonus to this book is the accompanying website – **www. MasteringTheArtOfTeamCoaching.com** – containing ancillary materials, articles, exercises and tools indicated by this symbol. This will give you a more interactive experience, encouraging you to follow up things you are particularly interested in. The links will be continually reviewed and updated to keep the book at the cutting edge of the discipline.

Finally, it would be remiss of me not to mention the growth of virtual team coaching. Many coaches and teams have limiting beliefs around what is possible when working online. They assume that you can't create the same degree of contact, connection and depth in virtual sessions. Some advocate that you must keep sessions short and use technology and tools to hold people's attention. Personally, I have found the opposite to be true and have experienced that you can achieve profound, emotional and rich learning experiences online. By creating a safe space and slowing things down, people can reconnect with themselves and each other. Almost all the concepts in this book are applicable to both co-located and online team coaching. For more on this subject, see Allard de Jong's article 'Team Coaching in a Virtual World' (de Jong, 2020) on the book website.

There is so much more to share and explore about the growing field of team coaching than I can offer in one book. If you would like to meet our faculty and growing community of team coaches around the globe, then join our free community of practice at **www.teamcoachingstudio.com**, where you can participate in online sessions on a broad range of related topics.

In short, you are holding in your hands a portal to the world of team coaching.

Welcome!

Georgina Woudstra, MCC

Team Coaching Studio

www.teamcoachingstudio.com

www.MasteringTheArtOfTeamCoaching.com

1 Teams Matter

It's not the team with the best players that wins but the players with the best team.

– ANON

As I write this, I am not alone in wondering what our future world will be like. We have never before experienced chaos on such a global scale. It feels eerily like sailing on a ship with nothing but sea for miles and miles and no land in sight. In this transitional space, we are aware that the shore from which we embarked is forever changed and the destination is unknowable. Some people thrive on living in the space between the past and the future; others are crippled by the uncertainty. One thing is clear to me: we are evolving into a new era. Organisations may still create three- to five-year plans, but they are likely to end up with very different results than they imagined as the future is no longer predictable.

Over the course of a few months, businesses went virtual. What was initially a temporary solution to help mitigate the spread of a virus brought a paradigm shift resulting in a lasting change in how people work, a change that requires us to learn and establish new ways of unleashing the power, purpose and potential of teams. A team can be like another family. Relationships grow, creating a sense of loyalty and belonging. We experience huge satisfaction from achieving more together than we can alone. The forming of human bonds happens organically in co-located teams – how will they form in a virtual world?

When our interactions become very transactional and all about tasks and getting stuff done, the heart and soul of human connection is stripped back. What is left is a form of Taylorism, in which workers become like machines in a factory, processing a series of tasks. A motivated and productive workforce needs to be sustained by finding meaning, belonging and engagement in their work, and this comes from human relationships combined with the opportunity to make a real difference.

The way to achieve this is through teams that are 'teaming' – fluid, creative and empowered to seize opportunities as they emerge. Teams can no longer be passive receptacles of the leader's decisions. Instead they must become partnerships formed to deliver value through collaboration and innovation. Team members are likely to be a blend of full-time employees, interims and freelance contractors. No longer constrained by geography, talent will be drawn from a global pool, and a defining factor in selection will be people's ability to collaborate as team players.

Teams and teaming will be more vital than ever before to organisational success. However, teams often struggle to fulfil their potential. Varied research reveals a narrative of underachievement, with as few as 10–20 per cent of teams operating as high performing. This is not surprising as teams are often thrown together and simply expected to work, which is akin to assembling a kitchen table load of the finest ingredients and expecting them miraculously to morph into a Michelin-star meal. The top kitchens in the world practise teamwork; everyone, from the chef down, knows their role, and they all need to work together to deliver culinary magic. Undeniably, the future of organisations is in the hands of teams, and team coaches are the key to turning up the dial of collaboration, which is the primary driver of team performance.

The power of collaboration

'Collaboration' has become a corporate buzzword, and for the good reason that it makes teamwork successful. Effective collaboration is the skill of working together to achieve a common purpose or goal. It happens when a group of people come together and contribute their creativity, knowledge and skills to make something happen. That 'something' needs to be *more* than individuals can achieve by themselves. If it isn't, it's a waste of everyone's time.

Most organisations recognise that teams are needed to achieve real results. But while it is relatively easy to take a group of brilliantly talented people and give them a collective task, it is by no means simple to get them to collaborate productively. When strong people are not aligned, they fragment, losing focus on collective outcomes, instead turning their attention to individual interests and goals. So, how well team members collaborate with other team members, and how well teams collaborate with other teams, will greatly impact the success of any project and therefore any organisation.

All projects experience roadblocks. A roadblock can be dismantled when a team use their collective wisdom, knowledge, skills and experience, reopening the road forward. Teams that collaborate learn from each other and learn together. Over time, the team's capability grows exponentially, along with their capacity to take on greater challenges.

Teams who work well naturally trust each other more, which makes for a more open, connected and engaged workplace. In turn, this boosts the morale of the team and other teams that they work with. And it goes without saying that a great culture is what attracts and retains the best people. We want to work with people we trust, where we feel valued and where we are making a worthwhile impact. Creating a collaborative workplace takes time, but the results are worth the effort. This happens by ensuring that all workplace teams transform from being blocks on an organisational chart to become units of collaboration.

What is a 'team'?

Corporations, NGOs and government departments are organised into teams, but it is important to understand what a team is to get the best out of them. In *The Wisdom of Teams*, Katzenbach and Smith (1993) define *real teams* in this way:

> A team is a small number of people with complementary skills who are committed to a common purpose, performance goals and approach for which they hold themselves mutually accountable.

This is a seminal definition, so it is worthwhile exploring the component parts:

Small number:

I have been asked to coach 'teams' with up to 25 members, although the majority have less than 10. Without much consideration or design, many leaders simply default to calling their group of direct reports a team. All too often, the result is teams with far too many chefs in the kitchen. Large groups have difficulty communicating effectively, let alone making decisions. Large 'teams' naturally split into subgroups rather than function as one team.

A *real team* is the optimum size to do its work. If a team needs to make strategic decisions, then research says that optimum membership is between five and eight. Less than five and the team may be short on the diversity of thinking needed for high quality debate and decision-making. More than eight slows decision-making right down, and the team quickly becomes a drag on the wings of the organisation. Large teams often resort to meetings based on information updates, with the leader left as the 'decision-maker'. In this situation, the leader can easily become a bottleneck, slowing workflow, creating inefficiency and frustrating team members and projects. Neither situation is likely to create the conditions for team effectiveness.

Complementary skills:

A *real team* has the skills needed to achieve its goals. There are three categories of skills:

➤ *Technical or functional:* the expert knowledge and skills necessary for their field – e.g. a management team in a software development firm is likely to need the complementary skills of engineering and marketing.

➤ *Problem-solving and decision-making:* including identifying problems, evaluating options and making decisions.

➤ *Interpersonal skills:* effective communication, constructive conflict, risk-taking, curiosity, support and challenge, all of which are vital to successful collaboration.

Team members are often recruited for their technical or functional expertise, and interpersonal skills are ignored. Yet too often team leaders complain: 'I have hired the strongest, smartest players in the field, so why can't they work together?' Fortunately, collaboration is a skill that can be learned; but some are better equipped for it than others.

Committed to a common purpose and performance goals:

If a team is not clear on its collective reason for being, its success will largely be down to chance. A meaningful and shared purpose is the driver, but often I hear a team leader asking why their team fails to 'gel' or become 'cohesive'. Yet, when asked about their purpose, the failing team are vague about it – or hide behind a form of words like 'to execute our business plan'.

Real teams coalesce around challenging aspirations and meaningful goals. With these clear, the projects and tasks they need to be collaborating on also become clear.

An *approach* for which they hold themselves *mutually accountable*:

By 'approach', Katzenbach and Smith mean well-developed ways of working. Don't fall into the trap of believing that a bunch of highly paid, smart people *should* naturally work together. The reality is very different, as without time and effort put into crafting and embedding ways of working, members are likely to switch their attention to more operational tasks run by their own departments or functions. Useful questions to explore are:

➤ Who leads on what?

➤ What skills might be missing? How will gaps be plugged?

➤ How will schedules be adhered to?

➤ What information does the team need? How will this be updated?

➤ How will decisions be made?

Of course, many more questions will need to be answered as the team evolves their working practices.

Decisions are pointless without accountability. Inexperienced or unconfident teams say – or think – 'the leader holds me accountable'; mature, effective teams say with confidence 'we hold ourselves accountable'. Without mutual accountability, there is no team. Katzenbach and Smith say:

> At its core, team accountability is about the sincere promises we make to ourselves and others, promises that underpin two critical aspects of teams: commitment and trust.

In *real teams*, each team member has the right to express their views about any aspect related to the team's work and to have their views listened to and considered.

A seat at the table

What gives a team member a right to a seat at the table? Just having a role in an organisational chart and a matching job title is not enough to play for the team. Being a member of the team should be as prized as being a member of Real Madrid or Manchester United football teams. So, what earns people a right to the seat, and how will continued membership be earned? Also, what will lose them a right to the seat?

Here are some questions you can ask teams to help them to assess whether they are, or even want to be, a real team:

➤ Are the team's boundaries clear? (e.g. does everyone know who is a team member and who isn't?)

➤ Is there sufficient stability for team members to learn to work effectively together over time? (Each change requires the team to reset.)

➤ What is the clear and compelling purpose for their work together as a team?

➤ Does the team have the right people, with the skills, knowledge and collaborative mindset needed to achieve their goals?

➤ What is the collaborative work that team members need to do to achieve their purpose?

➤ To what degree does the team leverage the knowledge, skills and strengths of each team member?

➤ Is the team collectively responsible for outcomes, i.e. 'none of us is successful unless the team is successful'?

➤ To what degree does the team collectively manage relationships with the wider system? (So often this is seen as the role of the team leader alone.)

➤ To what degree do members collectively manage team process, dynamics and relationships in the team? (Again, often pushed up to the team leader.)

When a new chief financial officer, Frank, joined the company, his initial focus was on a turnaround plan and making the numbers. He had restructured the team with some new recruits to join those who had been in the business for some time. Historically the FDs reported into divisional MDs and operated very much in their own silos. Now they reported to Frank and were required to start working together as one finance team.

As a function, finance was going through considerable change triggered by the Hackett building safety review, mainly around processes and common data warehousing. Individual senior leadership team members were heading up sub-projects around these changes, revealing issues on how the team worked together.

A previous off-site meeting was held on what they needed to focus on as a senior leadership team, and now they needed to establish how they were going to work together as a team. I was briefed by HR that there was a lack of open sharing and difficulties when an individual was required to compromise their own team for the good of the whole. There was also a tendency to go back over old ground in meetings, which slowed down the resolution of issues.

I was told that Frank was planning a two-day off-site for the team and was looking for a coach to support the team in:

➤ understanding what was holding the team back from consistently and reliably working together as 'one team'

➤ establishing how the senior leadership team was going to work together as a team (team norms)

➤ shifting members from parochialism to operating as one team

➤ encouraging team members to play to each other's strengths.

I began by conducting one-to-one interviews with each team member. Having originally been told that the team had 12 members, I was surprised when I was asked to interview 17 people. The interview data revealed that people were unclear who were 'official' team members and what their roles were; indeed, they knew little about each other. Additionally, they showed little appetite to get to know one another, seeing this as a waste of time. They said they were overwhelmingly busy and had 'enough work to do leading their own teams'. One respondent said he was unclear whether he was supposed to be working for Frank or for the MDs, who tended to see Finance as 'a necessary evil'.

There were many other points of data, the most significant being that they were unaware of any common objectives that required them to work together as a team. Within the business they were not perceived as a team but rather as small groups leading various functions within finance.

I asked the team in what ways might Frank be contributing to the team's effectiveness, or lack of it. I learned that he had grown increasingly frustrated at the lack of teamwork. He had a short attention span, regularly switching off and not listening. One team member told me: 'He continually blasts the team – bangs on the table, shouts and swears. I'm not sure this achieves what he hopes it will.' Another said: 'He tries to use scare tactics, threatening to fire people if they are not "performing".' This resulted in people watching their backs and playing safe, and they were certainly too afraid to approach him.

Despite the agreement that he would be in the session for the whole of the two days, as it was his team, he only turned up for the first hour, then said something important had come up and disappeared. I believe he felt that the team should work as a team because he told them to and that he had no further part to play. But the team members had no sense of themselves as a team and, understandably, no confidence in Frank as team leader.

What is the moral of this story? You can't coach a team to be a team when they see no reason to be one. Generally speaking, people are only willing to commit the time and effort necessary to work together as a team if they are compelled by meaningful outcomes.

As coach, it is not your responsibility to tell the client what makes a real team. But it usually helps to offer a framework of possibilities as food for thought. Using language that is fitting for the team you are working with can be much more effective than quoting the 'should book'. Here's a quote that often seems to hit the mark with teams who enjoy a more upbeat and aspirational concept of what makes a team. I might share this and then invite dialogue around what it means to the team:

TOGETHER EVERYONE
TEAM
ACHIEVES MORE

What happens in teams as they grow and change?

Teams grow and change over their lifecycle, and one of the best-known models for understanding what happens in groups is Tuckman's (1965) 'Stages of Group Development', otherwise known as 'Forming, Storming, Norming & Performing'. In the same era, Eric Berne (1963), the creator of transactional analysis, developed a theory of group process. Together they offer a comprehensive way of understanding the journey to team maturity and performance.

Berne says that there are two ways of mapping groups:

1   public structure – what everyone knows and sees about the group (therefore more behavioural)

2   private structure – what goes on inside each individual (therefore more about unexpressed or unaware thoughts and feelings).

He refers to this private structure as a group 'imago', an image or picture in our minds of any group we join or are part of. This imago is deeply personal, with roots in our first group experience, our family of origin. It is then shaped by our lived experience of groups we have participated in throughout life. Our experience of new groups is coloured by this image and all that it means to us. We arrive with an 'expected' image of what the group is or how it should be, based on a mixture of past experience and hope or fantasy.

We all have common needs when entering a group, the primary ones being:

➤ A need for *psychological safety* (which is often initially provided in groups by structure).

➤ A need for *familiarity*: a need to communicate and operate in a way that is familiar (otherwise thought of as group 'norms').

➤ A need for *stimulus*, provided by 'strokes' which Berne defines as 'units of recognition'. Think of this as how you give attention, perhaps through a look, a gesture or an interaction. Strokes provide stimulus to an individual, which is why we often haven't really entered a group and become present until we have either spoken or made direct and meaningful contact with another person.

➤ A need for *intimacy*, or social closeness.

Tuckman's model places more emphasis on what is happening at a behavioural level, which Berne refers to as the *public structure*. Berne helps us to understand what may be happening under the surface, in the *private structure*.

As time passes, groups develop through a process of adjustment which involves *differentiation* as individuals express their ideas, hopes and desires and through *group cohesion* where members seek to maintain harmony and familiarity. The process of adjustment is in four stages.

Let's look at the stages of development at both behavioural and psychological levels.

Stage One: Forming/Provisional Imago

Behavioural level: Each team member's focus is on the leader, seeking the leader's guidance and authority and maintaining a polite but distant relationship with others. The team is getting its bearings, and members are on their best behaviour. They meet to learn about goals and tasks and to get to know their colleagues. Discussion centres on projects and tasks, defining them and how to approach them.

Psychological level: At this stage individuals' focus is more on 'I' than 'we', and they are concerned with themselves and their relationship to the group leader. Unless already known to each other, other members are in one undifferentiated subgroup.

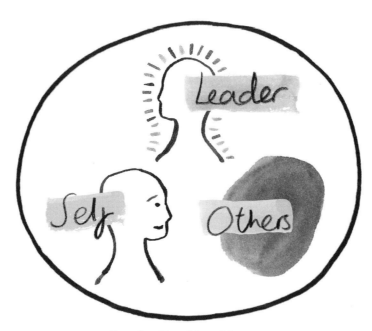

Forming/Provisional Imago

Individuals feel some anxiety about revealing too much of themselves, preferring 'safe' exchanges while internally keeping watch over the situation, trying to work out the 'the rules of engagement'. Members' relationships with the leader is a major preoccupation as, ultimately, they are heavily dependent on them. The leader is often subject to members' projections of what 'a leader' should be.

Leader's role: At this stage there needs to be someone who is clearly in charge. The leader may need to be more directive, providing clarity by setting the team's purpose and objectives, defining roles and expectations, and helping team members to see how they fit into the team. A skilled leader also invests time listening and seeking to understand, and role-models the values and behaviours they want to embed in the team.

Stage Two: Storming/Adapted Imago

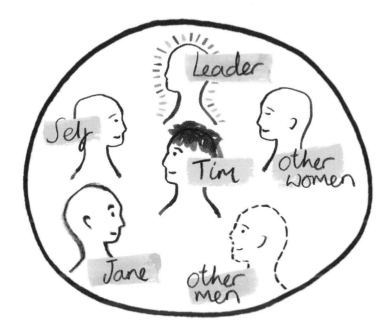

Adapted Imago

Behavioural level: Gradually team members start to show more of themselves, voicing different opinions. As people work with each other, they learn about individual working styles. Conflict may arise and 'storming' occurs, perhaps in the form of curt emails, sharp comments or put-downs in meetings. Members vie for the leader's attention, sometimes by seeking to add more value and sometimes, less helpfully, by running down colleagues. The leader's authority may also get challenged or tested, either openly or through passive behaviours like withdrawing, a lack of energy, lateness or non-attendance. This is the stage where silos and turf wars can develop as members seek to get decisions made outside of the room, as they are not yet sure what can be said in meetings, or what support they will get for their ideas. If the team doesn't grow beyond this stage, these silos can become deeply entrenched.

Psychological level: As time passes and people begin to feel safer in the group, a process of adjustment occurs. Individuals become more aware of other people and look for kindred spirits. People seek to find out more about other group members, talking about what matters to them and how they feel. Subgroups begin to naturally form, based around people who share ideas and values and with whom they feel the safest. This is an important stage, and the forming of subgroups is not one to disrupt as intimacy and trust is developing.

This is the stage when power struggles start to happen as members begin to express or act out more individual needs, which can collide with the team's need for cohesion. Berne called this the 'adapted imago' as members often act in the way they responded as children to parental authority and in sibling bonding and rivalry.

Leader's role: A skilful leader focuses team effort on building trust and dialogue, and surfacing and working through conflict, as this is the key to progressing on to the next stage. They let go of the small stuff and encourage people to do things their own way wherever possible.

Stage Three: Norming/Operative Imago

Operative Imago

Behavioural Level: Sadly, some teams never get beyond the storming stage. However, if they do reach the norming stage, they can begin to flourish. The team is more stable and should be making progress. Goals are clear and relationships are more established, enabling members to draw on each other's strengths and freeing members up to collaboratively make things happen. Team 'norms', or habits of behaving and working together, have become well established, so the team no longer needs to invest energy in how to get things done.

Psychological level: At this stage, team members are more differentiated, but there is also a much greater sense of 'we'. People are seen for who they are including their values, strengths, weaknesses and patterns of behaviour. It is OK to be themselves in the group 'warts and all'. They have developed some confidence in their ability to resolve disagreements and personality clashes, and great intimacy and a cooperative spirit emerges.

Each team has its own culture or personality: some might establish well-formed structures and rules, while others operate with spontaneity and creative chaos. Natural leaders have emerged, and leadership is therefore more distributed. This is an important stage where group cohesion is strong, the team's capacity has grown and effectiveness increases as subgroup working shares the load. However, the danger here is that members may be so intent on preserving harmony that they may be reluctant to oppose or challenge one another, potentially resulting in 'groupthink'.

Leader's role: At this stage, the leader can step back a bit and let team members assume more leadership in the team, although it's wise not to withdraw too much. Leaders need to keep stimulating healthy debate to help the team to develop further and reach the next stage.

Stage Four: Performing/ Secondarily Adapted Imago

Secondarily Adapted Imago

Behavioural level: With roles and norms established, the team focuses on achieving its collective purpose. Team members are competent, autonomous and able to handle decision-making without supervision. Now is the time for the team to stretch and challenge themselves by challenging the status quo and identifying the BHAGs, or 'big hairy audacious goals' (Collins & Porras, 1994).

Psychological level: Again, as time passes, team members become even more differentiated. Members can go beyond sharing thoughts and ideas, also being able to be vulnerable with one another, asking for help and offering support. Members feel a strong sense of belonging and empowerment and are able to focus their energy on achieving the team's purpose as they are not spending it on unhelpful conflict and game-playing. However, if goals are not defined that challenge and stretch members, the team can become too comfortable, gradually eroding motivation and satisfaction.

Leader's role: At this stage, the team can run interdependently, with minimum supervision from the leader. With the team now performing, the leader can focus more energy outwards and upwards, looking to outside influences, market drivers, competition, and so on. At the same time, the leader champions the team to take on bigger goals and meaningful groundbreaking work.

As discussed, relatively few teams are high performing. Supporting teams to collaborate effectively together towards what matters most is some of the most significant work that I can imagine. In many organisations, in the void of a purpose so compelling that our 'I' surrenders to the greater 'we', people focus on themselves and their personal goals and career aspirations. This fuels the conditions where organisations fail to harness the collective power of teams – and the potential that exists way beyond what any one person can do alone. This potential is not a dream, it has become an existential imperative, one that requires a future where every team has a coach partnering it to be the best it can be.

In the next chapter, we look more deeply into what this means and the role of the team coach. Dr Declan Woods will now guide you through your first reflection time.

Reflection time

What is the role and contribution of team coaching to the ever-changing nature of the world? Real change comes through new mindsets. What is your mindset as a team coach? Are you ready and brave enough for the messiness of real team coaching? If you are, let's begin.

This chapter sets out why teams matter more than ever. As practitioners, we are on the edge of an emerging field, helping to create and shape it. This is a perfect opportunity to think about what the world and teams need, and our place and contribution towards this as we pioneer together. Ask yourself:

➤ How do you foresee organisational life changing?

➤ What are the implications of this for your work with teams?

➤ How are you developing as a team coach for the future that is emerging?

➤ As we increasingly shift to virtual ways of working, how will you adapt? Do you understand the challenges of virtual 'teaming' and how technology can be used to enable this and for how you work with teams?

If teams truly matter, it is important that we have our own perspective on them as practitioners. Ask yourself:

➤ Why do teams matter?

➤ Why do you choose to work with them?

➤ Why do you want to be a team coach?

➤ What purpose or need (of yours) does this meet?

➤ What is your definition of a team?

➤ What makes a team a team?

➤ What makes an effective team?

With reference to Berne, draw an imago of:

➤ your first team (this could be your family of origin)

➤ your best team

➤ your worst team.

How are these similar and different? Are they linked? In what way(s)?

What are the implications of these imagoes on your beliefs about teams and your team coaching practice?

Think about the last team you worked in or led.

➤ What were your personal needs when joining this team?

➤ How do your personal needs in belonging to a team show up in your work with teams?

➤ What might this mean if you pay more or less attention to your own needs while team coaching?

➤ What are the implications of this for the roles you might play as a team coach? (We will look at this in more detail in Chapter 2.)

2 The Role of Team Coach

Not for the faint-hearted...

About 20 years ago, a CEO I was coaching asked whether I could work with his team. I thought this would be an exciting new challenge, so I agreed. To help me prepare, I bought all the books I could find on teams and facilitation, though I looked in vain for titles specifically on coaching teams. So I began running awaydays, mainly focused on helping team members to get to know each other better so that they could develop the mutual trust and respect on which all good teamwork depends. We crafted a statement defining the team's purpose, and developed a team charter determining how they would work together.

I mostly got great feedback, which was obviously gratifying, but so often these successful awaydays proved only a short-term fix. I became increasingly disillusioned when, a few months later, most teams had reverted to business as usual, forgetting their working agreements, not following through on actions and not holding each other to account. I didn't have this experience with my one-to-one coaching clients, so what was different? Individual clients blossomed in their confidence, focus, skill set, and so on. Why couldn't I achieve the same results with a team?

I turned to the wisdom of Sir John Whitmore (1997), a founder of our profession and what it means to be a coach, who says that 'coaching and high performance come out of *awareness* and *responsibility*'. Taking a coaching approach means helping the client to clarify their purpose, goals and agenda, and to raise the client's awareness of their situation and consider options – then helping them to define actions and develop their own structures of accountability.

I realised that I hadn't been coaching teams at all. I had slipped into a very different role: that of facilitator – the setter-up of awayday events, the person who made sure the whiteboard was clean and that there were enough pads and pencils to go round. I had fallen into facilitating teams when I needed to understand how to coach them. This was one of the most important realisations of my career, and I have spent the last two decades working it out.

As in all emerging fields there is significant confusion around what team coaching actually is. Comparable roles like consultant, trainer and facilitator get conflated with the role of coach, blurring important distinctions between them.

A definition of team coaching

Coaching has spread into all walks of life. There are countless schools and approaches used to support individuals who are looking for greater meaning and purpose in their lives. It is a tall order to define coaching in a way that offers clarity around the role and work of the coach while also embracing the very different approaches out there, such as performance coaching, solutions-focused coaching, brain-focused coaching, narrative coaching, integrative coaching, coaching for resilience and wellbeing, thinking partnership, systemic and gestalt. These are a drop in the ocean of possibilities available to coaches, and while some approaches claim to be better than others, there is no one right way. What works for one client won't work for another.

What binds all these together as a unified profession is a philosophy based on a core set of beliefs. The largest global professional body for coaching, the International Coaching Federation (ICF), advocates that coaching honours the client as the expert in his or her life and work, and believes that every client is creative, resourceful and whole. Standing on this foundation, the coach's responsibility is to:

➤ discover, clarify and align with what the client wants to achieve

➤ encourage client self-discovery

➤ elicit client-generated solutions and strategies

➤ hold the client responsible and accountable.

Coaching is distinct from other service professions, such as counselling, mentoring, consulting and training. It is a client-driven process, meaning the client chooses the focus of the conversation while the coach listens, asks questions and shares observations. The coaching interaction is designed to create awareness as a catalyst for learning and growth. Coaching accelerates the learning process by providing focus and increasing the client's options; the client is responsible for making choices and for taking any action. Coaching concentrates on where the client is in the here-and-now and how they get to where they want to be in the future. Results are a matter of the client's intentions, choices and actions stimulated by the coaching process.

The ICF defines coaching as: 'Partnering with clients in a thought-provoking and creative process that inspires them to maximize their personal and professional potential.'

So, with this in mind, what is team coaching?

Some of the definitions you may encounter are more prescriptive than the ICF definition and to varying degrees guide the coach to slip into an expert role, which is more the domain of consultants. At TCS, we believe that our definition provides sufficient flexibility to embrace different approaches while working to the client's agenda (i.e. the team) and honouring the principles and beliefs that underpin our profession:

> **Partnering with a team to unleash its collective power, purpose and potential to connect and collaborate.**

(Thanks to Silvia de Ridder for the addition of 'connection' which brings a very important human aspect to the definition.)

How the role of team coach differs from similar roles

> A team is not a problem that needs to be analysed and solved but a potential to be unfolded.

– DANIEL MEIER (2005)

Some say it doesn't matter what you call 'the work'. But it does. It sets the parameters of what we do and how we show up. Coaching, counselling, training, facilitation and consultancy all have their own distinct standards, training and professional bodies. The knowledge, skills and behaviours of each role are different, and each has a different intent. If you are not clear about your role, then the client won't be either and, most importantly, your impact will be diluted.

Role clarity is essential for coaches, the teams they coach and the organisations that sponsor the work. It guides our mindset and beliefs, our skills and competencies. Let's take the activities of each of four roles: consultant, facilitator, trainer and coach. The distinction between roles is clear, even across a wide variety of cultures, and can be tabulated in this way:

ROLE	BEHAVIOUR
CONSULTANT	Researching, diagnosing, analysing, advising, solving problems, presenting reports...
TRAINER	Developing curriculum, teaching concepts, skills, knowledge, strategies, tools...
FACILITATOR	Designing an agenda and managing the meeting process, allowing the team to focus on the content...
TEAM COACH	Partnering, holding the space, contracting, listening, questioning, direct communication, creating awareness, checking progress...

Different group interventions

When you allow the distinctions between the different roles to blur, you may find yourself taking on tasks that are actually *the team's responsibility*, such as making decisions, typing up notes of meetings, chairing meetings, recording actions and following up on progress. You also set client expectations and become seen as a jack of all trades. Once the client is used to you facilitating meetings, solving problems and offering solutions, they continue to look to you to perform these tasks. This may seem like a good idea in the short term, but it undermines the central need for the team to recognise, develop and own the skills it needs to perform at the highest level.

How do you avoid role confusion and inadvertently taking on too many tasks? First, get really clear on how you see the role of team coach. Then decide whether you are prepared to play related roles. If so, ask yourself what the drivers are for you to play these additional roles, what boundaries will you set around each role and how will you signal each shift in role?

Note, the fact that your client may ask you to play these roles isn't necessarily a reason to do so. We can easily get sucked into filling voids in the team when the gap really needs to be filled by a team member.

A recent supervisee told me she had recently found herself agreeing to put together a RACI (responsible/accountable/consulted/informed – a chart for identifying roles and responsibilities) for the team. On reflection, she felt pulled into organising this because there appeared to be significant duplication and confusion around who owned various projects and tasks. On delving deeper, she became aware of a leadership void, where there was a lack of clarity on goals and priorities as well as roles and accountabilities. Instead of taking on this leadership task herself, she coached the team leader to do this, thereby building greater leadership capacity for the future.

Process versus content

> As a team coach, I'm more interested in the 'how' than in the 'what'.

The roles which become the most muddled are facilitator and coach. However, these are different roles with a clear and distinct purpose. A facilitator manages the 'process' of a meeting or event (how they work together) enabling team members to focus on the 'content' (the task in hand). The aim of facilitation is usually to arrive at an 'instrumental outcome', in other words, concluding a task – like defining a vision and strategy for the organisation, making a critical decision or solving a problem.

Team members need to work on content together all the time and, to be effective as a team, they need to develop their capacity to manage the process for themselves. A team coach's aim is to help the team raise their awareness and ownership of their process, thereby guiding them on a path of learning how to manage themselves more effectively and more autonomously. We call this 'giving the process back to the team'.

Agreeing a vision or making a decision are incredibly useful outcomes for a team; however, if they use a facilitator whenever they need to make decisions as a team, they are not learning how to manage themselves more effectively.

Gallwey (2000) in *The Inner Game of Work*, offers a simple formula around human performance and what gets in the way: Performance = Potential – Interference, or P = P – I. In teams, the most common 'interference' is how they work together as a team, such as:

➤ how they structure and manage meetings

➤ how they engage in dialogue

➤ how they make decisions

➤ how they engage with stakeholders

➤ how they engage with other teams

➤ how they work with ambiguity and change

➤ how they challenge and support one another

➤ how they hold each other to account

➤ how they consciously and continually learn as a team.

The idea of 'process and content' is integral to an understanding of the role of the team coach. It derives from the work of Kurt Lewin, a social psychologist who did intensive research on the functioning of groups during the 1940s. He observed hundreds of groups and found that most were what he called excessively 'task-mesmerized'; in other words, they were inordinately preoccupied with whatever the task was that they were trying to accomplish but paid little or no attention to how they were going about it, often resulting in ineffective 'task processes' or ways of working. He realised that most of the problems that groups encountered were not to do with the actual task but the way that they were going about accomplishing it. Successful groups were the ones that intentionally managed both the content and process – the *what* and the *how*.

So, when a facilitator works with a team, it is no wonder that the team becomes more effective because the facilitator is managing the team's process. However, the team is not actually becoming more effective *as a team* – i.e. growing members' capacity to collaborate to achieve collective outcomes. To grow their collaborative horsepower as a team, they need to excel in the process of working together without the need for a facilitator to manage this for them.

Yet, without realising it, so many coaches morph into facilitators when working with teams. So we could say that, while a 'typical team coach' manages the team's process – by designing a workshop and bringing content (like assessments and exercises) – a great team coach becomes curious about the team's processes, generating awareness and responsibility in the team for effective teamwork. In this way, the team learns to become much more powerful and purposeful, and performs better as a team.

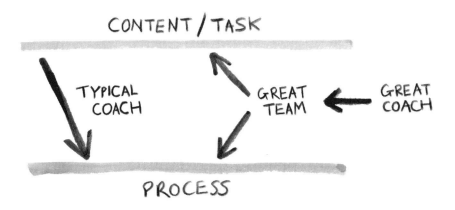

Coaching a team is often initially slower than facilitating a team, but the gains far outweigh the investment of time. Team coaching is about slowing the team down, in order to actually speed it up.

'We are looking for a team coach to work with the leadership team of our engineering division,' said the HR director. 'The team has been through a turbulent year; they are ground down and taking it out on each other, so their interpersonal relationships could use some work.' Further discussion revealed that the organisation intended to provide team coaching for mission-critical teams across the business to drive up performance. Additionally, they wanted each team to follow the same step-by-step approach, beginning with a prescribed set of assessments, followed by a two-day workshop where they would receive feedback on the assessments and work through a sequence of sessions on team purpose, goals, leadership styles and building trust.

When you read this brief, what role do you think the team is really looking for? In my view they are looking for a team facilitator. Here's why:

1. **The work was mandatory, not voluntary. The voluntary nature of coaching is part of our ethical code as coaches, and it is essential for building trust and engagement in the coaching process. Team coaching puts the responsibility for acting on the learnings from coaching sessions on the team.**

2. It was a one-off event. Coaching is a journey that takes place over time. Why? Because human beings don't learn, change or grow overnight. The same applies to teams, magnified to the power of ten.

3. The work was not at all co-creative or mutual. It was all designed by the HR team, and the team were subject to this design. This is hardly likely to create a sense of ownership and empowerment.

I am not saying that any facilitation of this team will be a waste of time. However, if the desired outcome is improved teamwork, resulting in higher performance, then they will need more than a facilitated workshop.

So, the next time you are invited to 'coach' a team and the leader gives you a brief for an awayday and says the team need to get to know each other better and to become more cohesive as a team, what will you do?

Different team interventions

When you get an enquiry for team coaching, it is helpful to be able to recognise what the client is asking for so that you can match your work to the need. Also, many organisations are not at all clear on what team coaching is, so they may ask for it as it's become a popular term, but their frame of reference and therefore their expectation is actually team development or facilitation.

Group Coaching	Team Facilitation	Team Building	Team Development	Team Process Coaching	Team Coaching	Live Action Coaching
Coaching individuals in a group context, such as in an action learning set.	Managing the process of a meeting, freeing the team up to focus on the task in hand.	Helping a team to form in the early stages of its development.	Developing a team to progress through the stages towards team maturity.	Providing reflection on and improving how the team is functioning.	Specific team coaching sessions, usually focusing on the team's learning objectives.	Coaching the team from the sidelines, in the here-and-now, while the team goes about its normal business.

Team interventions

Looking at this table, you can see that each intervention is quite distinct. Many books describe 'team coaching' as all of the above. Personally, I prefer greater clarity on what it is I am there to do as this means I am more likely to be successful.

Group coaching: Here the focus is on the learning and development of the individuals in the group. The individual experience is enhanced by learning in a group context. This is akin to most training courses where, as a participant, you have your own learning goals and outcomes and you are also part of a learning group. Group coaching is growing in popularity as it is often more effective and economical than providing one-to-one coaching across a company. I know of several organisations using group coaching right now to support leaders in varied developmental agendas like agility, resilience, virtual leadership, women leaders and change.

Group Coaching	Team Coaching
The clients are the individuals in the group. They are receiving coaching in a group setting and benefitting from sharing with others.	The client is the team and not the individuals who make up the team. The team is benefitting from the focus on the team as a whole.
The goal is the development and learning of the individuals in the group.	The goal is the development and learning of the team.

Team facilitation: I have already discussed this extensively. The origin of *facilitation* means 'the act of making something easier'. When facilitating the team, you are making their work easier by managing the process of how they work together on their behalf.

Team building: This is about helping a team to form. Often, this involves some sort of 'team launch', enabling team members to get to know one another better and creating a team charter where the team's purpose, vision, goals, roles, values and norms are agreed. Norms are sometimes referred to by other names, like 'working agreements', 'operating procedures', 'ground rules' or, my favourite, 'golden rules'.

Team development: Here you are coaching the team through the stages of team maturity. This could be Tuckman's 'forming, storming, norming, performing', Berne's 'group imago', Declan Woods' teamSalient stages of team development model (see www. teamsalient.com) or 'punctuated equilibrium' (Gersick, 1988). Which you choose depends on what makes most sense to you and the teams that you are working with.

Team process coaching: Here you are enabling the team to reflect and improve on how they are working together. The work is often focused around identified team learning goals, such as effective meetings, dialogue, decision-making and working through conflict.

Live action coaching: This is a very powerful intervention where you are coaching a team, in the here-and-now, while they are going about their normal business together. In this sense the teams are 'on the pitch' and you are on the sidelines. Your focus depends on the contract for the session and the learning goals of the team; however, it is likely to include making and sharing observations and inviting the team to experiment with new ways of working together.

Ultimately, you will decide how you define team coaching and the range of interventions that you offer. I hope this encourages you to think through the distinctions between each one and the implications for your role in them.

Reflection time

This chapter sets out the different types of intervention or modalities when working with teams and the roles we can take up and play, including as team coach.

As role clarity is vital for effective team coaching, let us reflect on this. What is your experience of working with groups and teams to date? Write your experiences down and note the roles you carried out. What do you notice?

➤ Which roles did you take up – and why was this?

➤ Which roles did you not take up – and why was this?

➤ If you are not facilitating or team consulting, what are you doing with a team?

➤ How has the pattern of roles you carried out changed:

    ➤ over time?

    ➤ within any one engagement or piece of work with a group or team?

    ➤ did these changes in role just happen or were they an active choice? What informed that choice?

Considering your team coaching philosophy (we will cover this in more detail in Chapter 3). What are your beliefs about:

➤ teams

➤ team development?

➤ change

➤ the role of the team coach?

Reflect upon your pre-coaching experience of working in an organisation.

➤ What influences do you draw upon from this experience that informs your work with teams now?

➤ What else informs your thinking about teams?

➤ What else informs your team coaching practice with teams?

3 The Tao of Team Coaching

The mystery of human existence lies not in just staying alive, but in finding something to live for.

– FYODOR DOSTOYEVSKY, *The Brothers Karamazov*

Over the last 20 years, coaching has proved one of the fastest-growing professions worldwide. It has become integral to the fabric of organisations as an approach for developing leaders, improving cultures and accelerating growth. It has also become a style of leading and managing, a dramatic shift from the 'command and control' leadership of the past. We now see the need to cultivate leadership throughout organisations and unlock people's potential to boost their own performance. We do this by helping people to think for themselves and enabling them to learn rather than spoon-feeding them. As Sir John Whitmore says, 'After all, how did you learn to walk? Did your mother or father instruct you? We all have a built-in, natural learning capability that is actually disrupted by instruction.'

Coaching works because of the unique nature of the relationship between coach and client – a partnership. Unlike a mentor, whose role is to impart all they know, the best coaches do not need to have a wealth of expertise in what the client wants to learn. Indeed, too much knowledge can undermine the dynamic of the partnership, placing the practitioner in a 'one-up' position passing down knowledge to the client, the recipient of this wisdom. Instead, as a coach you are an expert in coaching, not in the subject at hand. In essence, the coaching relationship is a collaborative partnership created to discover and awaken the client's potential.

These days, most well-trained executive coaches have learned to embody this coaching mindset in their work. For some reason, team coaching has slipped through the net. Many 'team coaches' are practising something very different from coaching as I would define it. But I can relate to this, and the following account of an experience from earlier in my career will demonstrate how easy it is to stray.

As the new millennium got into swing, I found myself increasingly getting asked to do some team coaching. I was excited, as this presented fantastic opportunities to work with new clients in a whole variety of sectors. At the same time, I was struck by fear. What were they expecting of me? What was I supposed to do? What if it didn't work?

I was not alone in this experience. Many coaches have shared with me the stomach-churning dread of working with a new team. I don't believe that team facilitators are afflicted in the same way because their role carries the expectation of leadership. I wanted to feel more competent and in control and was looking for anything that would stop my knees knocking and my mouth going dry. So I hunted for a miracle cure in the form of tools, models and exercises that would guide my work and lead, of course, to amazing results.

In my quest, I discovered a brilliant fable on team dysfunction. It was the story of a leader needing to unite a team before it brought the company to its knees. The story was so compelling and the model so simple and clear. This would be my magic wand. I found the author's website and, to my delight and at great expense, I purchased their whole kit in a box!

At the first opportunity that presented itself, I put it to work. The kit had it all: handbooks for team members, a workshop agenda with timings, exercises and supporting slides. To my amazement, it even came with a facilitator script.

The workshop was taking place in a beautiful countryside mansion, set in acres of parkland with mature trees, lakes and manicured gardens. Inside, there were wood-panelled rooms with open fires and plush upholstery. The five-star service was immaculate, and I was escorted to our event suite, which was grand while also having the relaxed feel of a weekend retreat. The environment was perfect, I was all kitted up and I finally felt in control.

The day got off to a great start with everyone arriving on time and in a positive mood. The CEO opened the session answering to the purpose of the workshop and why now. They had formed as a team a year ago, but he believed they could work more effectively together: they were not good enough at prioritising and the pace they were operating at was unsustainable.

I followed, outlining the agenda for the two days, as prescribed in the kit. The day would start with a look at the team dysfunctions model and we would then review the results of a team assessment which each member had completed prior to the workshop. After this, we would work through the elements of the model, starting with building trust.

The team were relatively engaged during my 20-minute walk through of the model. They asked some questions, and I responded well. I was on a roll. Then we looked at the results of the team assessment. There was an hour in the agenda for this, which seemed like a good amount of time. The assessment revealed that the team scored low on trust, and that team members did not acknowledge their weaknesses to each other, apologise to each other, admit mistakes or ask each other for help. After giving them ten minutes to read through the report individually, they then spent another 15 in pairs discussing the results before each pair would share ideas for improving their results in plenary. I asked the first pair to share their reflections and recommendations. One person spoke for them and offered a lengthy monologue, critiquing the report and making recommendations for how the report could be improved. I asked what insight they had on their team, and they responded that the report wasn't representative and repeated their critique.

Over the next hour other team members joined in to play the same game, and I fell into the trap of defending the model and the assessment tool. I felt that I needed it to be right as the rest of the two days was designed around elements of the model. I felt my credibility and confidence slipping away, and my thoughts turned to how many more hours there were to the end of the day.

In the lunch break, I had some time to breathe and think. I realised that in using the kit I was completely trapped inside my head. I had disconnected from the team, and from myself and my inner coach. I resolved to change course and opened the afternoon session with an apology, followed by a check-in. I began to connect with the team and build trust. From this space I was able to coach the team on what they wanted from the session, rather than what I wanted for them.

I learned that the idea of having a complete kit with a pre-designed workshop was not team coaching; nor was it 'me'. While the dysfunctions model was truly groundbreaking, instead of looking for a 'guaranteed' step-by-step process, I needed to develop the art of working in the moment and meeting a team where they are at.

Real team coaching is about going beyond pre-planned agendas, tools and techniques into the process of 'safe emergence' (Fritz Perls, 1951). To do this, you must be able to create a safe-enough container to meet every moment and work emergently with the team in service of learning in the here-and-now – just as you would in one-to-one coaching. Mastery as a team coach is when these skills are in the bones, guiding your every thought and move. Team coaching becomes a unique expression of you and a practice that is truly congruent with who you are.

Being a team coach

> The moon does not fight. It attacks no one. It does not worry. It does not try to crush others. It keeps to its course, but by its very nature, it gently influences. What other body could pull an entire ocean from shore to shore? The moon is faithful to its nature and its power is never diminished.
>
> – DENG MING-DAO, *Everyday Tao*

What will it take for you to become a real team coach? What do you need to learn be able to create a safe-enough container and to 'sit in the fire' with a team when the heat is building? What do you need to meet each moment as it unfolds without needing to change or control it? What do you need to believe to give yourself permission to *be* a team coach rather than *do* team coaching?

Ancient principles in Taoism are concerned with observing the natural patterns and movement of nature and adjusting yourself to this flow. Similarly, the team coach is observing and working with the unfolding patterns, helping the team to adjust to an ever-changing flow.

The work of a real team coach comes from the heart. It emanates from a deep trust in yourself and in the coaching process. This requires you to know yourself – what you believe in and stand for. Kets De Vries (2018) says 'the purpose of life is a life of purpose'. We stand for things that we consider worthwhile. When we are involved in something worthwhile, we come alive. We devote energy and time to it, and what we are doing becomes an expression of something that truly matters. When what you do matters, you are creating value – and this is the work of a team coach.

When you are in harmony with your unique way of *being*, you have a sense of ease in your work, your skills flow and you feel more effective. You become freer and more animated; and the fullest range of your presence becomes available to you. The critical voices in your head fall quiet – the ones that tell you that you should know more, do more, be more skilful – enabling you to tune into the here-and-now moment.

Knowing yourself comes from understanding your philosophy and your perception of reality, or 'world view'. As a coach, you need a personal philosophy or you risk responding to random stimuli and information without any clear intention as to the impact. Your philosophy is a set of principles that guide your work. It frames your perspective when noticing, listening or asking questions and it informs your body language, tone, style and choice of words. Your principles are something you stick to, even if they challenge you to your core. In the end, your principles will pay off because they provide a structure and momentum that enable connection and progress to happen.

A philosophy of team coaching

What then avails to guide us? One thing, and one alone — Philosophy.

– MARCUS AURELIUS, *Meditations*

As discussed, your philosophy of team coaching is deeply personal as it is an expression of what you find meaningful. Philosophy can seem like an esoteric doctrine, so it helps to form your philosophy into a set of principles as a frame of reference – a window through which you look at your clients and their situations.

Here are the core principles that guide me as a team coach:

1. **People are naturally creative, resourceful and whole**

2. **Teams are more than the sum of their parts**

3. **Teams are living entities with an innate collective wisdom**

4. **Effective teams creatively adjust to ever-changing circumstances**

5. **Exploration of the here-and-now experience creates awareness**

6. **Awareness is curative – once we become aware of something, we have the choice to change it**

7. **Individual and collective responsibility for change unleashes potential**

8. **Changes happen through active experimentation**

9. **Team capacity grows when they own their agenda and manage their own processes**

10. **What is possible depends on the situation and context, the collective awareness and responsibility of the team and the interior condition of the intervener.**

1. People, and teams, are naturally creative, resourceful and whole

People are not broken, and they don't need fixing. When we see people or teams as problems to solve, we diminish their potential and their power. Instead, we become the powerful one with the know-how to make them successful. This grandiose approach often says more about the ego of the coach than it does about the client. Teams can determine what success is for themselves, and they can find their own answers. And, if they really want to be given solutions, they can hire an advisor or consultant.

2. Teams are more than the sum of their parts

Babe Ruth said, 'The way a team plays as a whole determines its success. You may have the greatest bunch of individual stars in the world, but if they don't play together, the club won't be worth a dime.' A team becomes more than a collection of people when a strong sense of mutual commitment and the need for collaboration create synergy, generating greater performance than that possible from the sum of individual members.

3. Teams are living entities with an innate collective wisdom

Like an octopus, a team has lots of arms, and they are constantly on the move. Each arm contains its own 'brain' and is able to act independently. The octopus also has a central 'brain' which makes the octopus one entity. In a team, this 'entity' contains the identity, values and patterns of behaviour of the team. A team has its own collective intelligence that emerges from collaboration and collective efforts.

4. Effective teams creatively adjust to ever-changing circumstances

The world around us is constantly changing and, like white water rapids, it is turbulent and unpredictable. Great teams learn to navigate the moving and dynamic waters with increasing effectiveness. They grow their capacity and capability each time they complete a stretch of the river. They meet challenges; sometimes the boat overturns, but they get back upright and head off again, ever stronger and more agile.

5. Exploration of the here-and-now experience creates awareness

Making meaning, discovering what we need, making choices, taking decisions and finding new solutions happen in the now. Much greater awareness is created and responsibility is taken when we stay grounded in real experience. While is it vital to understand the importance of people's past experiences, the key is in understanding how they are impacting the present.

6. Awareness is curative – once we become aware of something, we have the choice to change it

We can only change what we are aware of; what we are unaware of sometimes controls us. Awareness is empowering and gives rise to insight and learning. Seeing our role as 'awareness agents' brings clarity and a sense of purpose to our work. The art of team coaching becomes awareness itself; the artistry is found in how each coach's presence and use of self transforms the awareness into meaningful change.

7. Individual and collective responsibility for change unleashes potential

The team's ability to reach its potential depends on the way its members work together and the degree to which they share objectives, values, purpose and responsibility. Teams that thrive take responsibility for creating the conditions for team effectiveness. Responsibility is a state of mind, and it starts with becoming more aware. When we take responsibility for our thoughts, decisions, actions and behaviour, our commitment to them increases, along with the focus and staying power to see things through.

8. Changes happen through active experimentation

Transformation begins with becoming aware of the potential for change, trying something new, learning from it and turning it into something sustainable and more productive. Essentially, life is a series of experiments, all of which invite new ways of thinking and being in the world. Just thinking about change changes nothing. Shifting from 'talking about' to real-time application is where the rubber meets the road.

9. Team capacity grows when they own their agenda and manage their own processes

If the coach leads the process of the team's dialogue or task and leads the direction of the questions, this will undermine the team's own responsibility and learning. So get out of the way and follow the team's own agenda.

10. What is possible depends on the situation and context, the collective responsibility of the team and the interior condition of the intervener

In team coaching results are not guaranteed. Sometimes the outcomes that a team is looking for are like asking a chef to create a Michelin star meal for 50 people with a box of six eggs. The conditions that influence the field of possibilities the most are a) the wider context, such as advances in technology or market forces, b) the culture of the organisation and team, c) a mindset of collective responsibility for awareness, meaning-making and action and d) the interior condition of you, the intervener, and your capacity to remain calm, clear and present.

The principles above are my own. I now invite you to consider and develop your own set of guiding principles.

What's your philosophy?

First why and then trust.

– SIMON SINEK, TEDx talk

Your philosophy of team coaching is your world view. Philosophy challenges us to evaluate our ideas and the beliefs that underpin our practice. This process can be uncomfortable, often surfacing more questions than answers. But the payoff can be enormous as it brings a clarity of purpose and coherence to our practice.

As a team coach, what is your philosophy of human relationships, interactions, learning and change? Ultimately, knowing your philosophy is about knowing your values and what is important to you. I urge you to also examine the philosophy that underpins the coaching profession and to consider your own values and how both inform your practice as a team coach.

Matthew is adamant that team coaching is all about accelerating team performance. A former professional athlete, from an early age his life has been defined by his own performance. His dedicated parents transported him at the crack of dawn to training on the track, and again after school. They sacrificed their own social life, interests and hobbies in service of his progress, never missing a day. Matthew's coaches set him goals that challenged him to the core, measuring his progress with a rigorous set of diagnostics that provided detailed insight into opportunities for improvement.

After retiring from a successful sporting career, Matthew believed his experience would transfer well to the workplace. He trained as a coach with a school whose primary focus was on results. Over time, he honed an approach which begins with setting outrageously stretching goals and then breaking these down into achievable chunks. He works with belief systems and how humans sabotage their own success. Around five years into his career as a coach, Matthew joined a management consultancy focused on the pursuit of excellence, working as a coach on their 'high-performing teams' programme offering a 'proven approach for accelerating team performance'. He describes seven key principles that govern his work:

1. High performing teams are not normal.

2. They are 100% clear on their goals and roles.

3. They get a plan in place and commit to it.

4. They put the team first, creating and maintaining a climate of trust and respect.

5. They achieve goals by overcoming obstacles and barriers and their immunity to change.

6. Great leadership is about providing direction, resolving conflicts and increasing cooperation.

7. The coach's role is to help them play at their best, both individually and as a team.

In defining these key principles, Matthew is expressing his beliefs about what creates success. As you can see, this is based on a lifetime of his personal experience, starting as a young child on the track. Personally, it is also about his own desire to perform – if the teams that he coaches are successful, then by default he is also successful.

Identifying your own guiding principles is likely to require cycles of reflective practice and self-inquiry. Rather than a tick-box exercise or a checklist activity, commit to a deeper questioning of your own assumptions about human nature, change, leadership, collaboration, power and any other aspects which underpin and define your practice. See the reflective questions at the end of this chapter to help you to develop your own set of questions.

Your stance as a team coach

Presence is defined as: the living out of values in such a way that in 'taking a stance', the intervener teaches these important concepts.

– EDWIN C. NEVIS (1987)

Your philosophy informs your stance, and together they shape you and your role as a team coach. They provide a compass along the journey, guiding how you relate to your work and to those around you.

Whereas your philosophy is about a set of principles or values that you hold dear, your stance is about taking a stand and acting on your values. Your stance, therefore, takes ideas and turns them into action. A team coach's stance often takes the form of a set of mantras that determine certain behaviours and skills. So, your stance is literally about *taking a stand*.

Here are some example mantras:

MANTRAS TO GUIDE YOUR STANCE AS A TEAM COACH

1. Follow the client's (team's) agenda

2. Trust the process

3. Contact before contract

4. Tune in

5. Be curious

6. Hold the space

7. Evoke awareness

8. Provoke experimentation

9. Focus on the here-and-now

10. Model collaborative behaviour

11. Embrace not knowing and go with the flow

12. Dance in the moment.

Follow the client's agenda: Coaching is an emergent process: the client (the team) sets the agenda, and this defines the work undertaken by the team coaching relationship. So, rather than you planning an agenda for a team coaching session, invite the team to define their learning or change agenda and coach the team towards these outcomes.

Trust the process: Trusting the process is about accepting your vulnerability because it calls upon you to trust the team to do the work. It is normal for a team to get frustrated when they don't have it all figured out, when there are power struggles or when they are not aligned. Team coaching is about creating awareness and building capacity, confidence and competence, and this happens over time, from week to week. You can try to speed through the team coaching in order to 'accelerate team performance', yet this often gets in the way of learning and growth.

So, let go of rescuing and stepping in to lead and take control. Let go of certainty because, in the presence of a team which is momentarily lost, it can be agonisingly tempting to step in and provide a pathway and a torch. Trusting the process means trusting your intuition, trusting questions, trusting the team's innate wisdom. Be optimistic and have faith that frustration can become the fountain of creativity.

Contact before contract: Learning requires us to take risks and to go beyond what is known. Naturally, people don't take risks if they don't feel safe. Making contact with others increases psychological safety and trust. This is essential. While new knowledge and awareness can be extremely helpful to a team, the team will only learn if they are open to risk-taking and engaged in the coaching partnership. Don't underestimate the time it takes to make contact with individuals and the team as a whole. If you try to contract with a team for change when you do not have good contact with them, the drawbridges will come up, making it impossible to create awareness or any meaningful change.

Tune in: Pay attention to what you are noticing. Tune in to your own feelings, the emotional reactions of team members and your 'felt sense' of the team. To do this you must get out of your head and into your heart. Tuning in is a practice; many people live in their heads, either blocking or numbing their senses. As babies we were able to feel – in fact it was our primary modality – and somewhere along the way we shut down. If you are struggling to connect with your emotions, then seek a therapist or a coach to support you in reconnecting with yourself.

Be curious: Humans are meaning-making creatures. Few can tolerate not knowing, so we fill in the blanks about what something means. For example, you are observing a meeting between a team of four and you notice that the leader has been talking most of the time, rather loudly and emphasising words with a lot of emotion. You notice the non-verbal communication between two members, who are frequently glancing at each other rolling their eyes. The fourth member is very quiet and expressionless. Naturally, you might have thoughts like this:

➤ The leader is so dominant, they are blocking others.

➤ Those two are like school kids, acting out passive-aggressively.

➤ The fourth member is intimidated; I want to bring her in, so she has a voice.

Like it or not, we all judge and interpret people and situations. However, we can choose how we react to our own inner dialogue. Where possible, resist offering interpretations and instead be curious.

Hold the space: This is one of the most profound interventions as a team coach because space is about being, not doing. In team coaching, we hold a space in which is it safe to be ourselves and to be real. When holding a space, you are communicating, through your thoughts and deeds, that 'It is OK to be you; it is OK to be us; we can be with whatever comes up.' When holding a space, you are able to notice any anxiety that the team is arousing in you. You are able to sit with it patiently – what we call 'sitting in the fire', allowing what needs to be surfaced to emerge into awareness.

Evoke awareness: Awareness creates choice and responsibility, and both are essential for change. Awareness arises naturally from the team's 'process' – their way of being and working together in each moment. If we stop controlling a team's process through facilitating exercises and activities and 'get out of the way', the team's process will naturally emerge.

Provoke experimentation: The crux between awareness and change is experimentation. Experimenting means taking risks; it means breaking out of the comfort zone of habitual behavioural patterns, even if those habits are ineffective. Taking risks requires an experimental attitude and being willing to try something different. Organisations often do this by creating pilots or hothousing an idea or process. Yet, teams rarely use this approach to change unhelpful patterns of behaviour. As a team coach, you are inviting the team to disrupt their habits and to 'try something'. Use an evocative presence to hold the space and to surface awareness, then shift to a provocative presence to stimulate experimentation.

Focus on the 'here-and-now': Learning happens when awareness is transformed into change. The pivotal moment between awareness and change is created through active experiments. Building on the notion of creating awareness, let's think about what we can become aware of. We can create awareness around many topics, and we can do this by looking at the past, the future or the here-and-now.

Imagine that a team you are coaching wants to improve their decision-making.

You can take them back into the past: What is a decision you previously made as a team? How did you go about making that decision?

Or you can prompt them towards the future: How can you improve your decision-making in your next meeting?

Or stay in the here-and-now: Let's experiment! Name a significant decision that you need to make as a team. The experiment has two steps: first, agree a process by which you are going to make the decision; second, put the process into action and see what happens.

Model collaborative behaviour: One of the ways we learn is by observing what is role-modelled to us. We pick up ways of expressing ourselves, ways of dealing with conflict and stress, ways of getting stuff done. Not all that we learn is ideal. Many people have not grown up in households where collaboration was the norm, and this lack of interaction to achieve positive outcomes can impact adult life and the world of work. Role-modelling collaborative behaviour is a powerful intervention in itself. Openly demonstrate working through differences, solving problems, giving and taking leadership, being curious, building on ideas and making decisions. Working in a team coaching pair gives you a fabulous opportunity to role-model these skills by openly negotiating with the team as your witness.

Embrace not knowing and go with the flow: Very much connected to trusting the process, *not knowing* means having a profound belief that the team knows better than you what is best for the team. Staying with not knowing can be tough, and it requires you to strengthen your 'not-knowing muscle'. Like going to the gym, the more you build the muscle, the more it's there for you when you need it. Building the 'not-knowing muscle' is helped by:

➤ putting models and theories to one side

➤ not making interpretations or assumptions

➤ tolerating ambiguity and messiness

➤ being surprised by the team

➤ being open to your own learning

➤ being self-aware; understanding your biases and proclivities.

Taking a not-knowing stance levels the playing field; it reduces the power difference between coach and team and invites the team to think and behave for themselves.

Dance in the moment: A simple phrase that says a lot. Sometimes you will be dancing a waltz, which has a predetermined form; other times, you move fluidly in response to the music. Yet, for many, learning to repeat the moves of a specific dance is easier than dancing freestyle. As with any art, fluidity of movement develops with practice. Dancing in the moment requires well-developed empathic responsiveness: a congruent *affective* (feeling- and emotion-based) response to the team or team members' experience or state. People know when this happens because they feel 'met'.

The above are examples of mantras which form part of my own team coaching stance. They may be useful to you, or they may not. For instance, my colleague, Allard de Jong, has a mantra 'stay loose', which reminds him to be in the moment and to ease up on his need to tighten up and focus on the timetable or agenda. I encourage you to do the reflective and inner work in order to create mantras that are congruent with who you are and how you practise as a team coach. Your mantras are there to support and guide you in every moment of your work.

Reflection time

You can begin by thinking about your life experience so far; dig deep to discover what lies beneath your answers to questions like:

➤ What attracted you to coaching in the first place?

➤ What difference did you hope to make to others and the world by becoming a coach? How is this similar or different for you as a team coach?

➤ What are your beliefs about humanity?

➤ Who has inspired you along the way?

➤ What ideas or concepts have inspired you and influenced your work?

➤ What are your values?

➤ Which books have been the most significant to you?

➤ What do you yearn to learn?

➤ What are your assumptions about change?

➤ What are your beliefs about teams, leadership and the role of the team leader(s)?

➤ What are your beliefs about the roles of team members?

➤ What are your beliefs about the role of the team coach?

➤ What are your assumptions about: decision-making, managing performance, responsibility, accountability within teams?

➤ When I say the word 'power', what thoughts or feelings arise in you? What does this tell you about your relationship with power?

For all or any of these questions, ask yourself 'Why do I believe that?' or 'Where does this come from?' Notice any responses that come from a 'should' voice as these might be someone else's beliefs or commands that you have 'swallowed whole' from someone in authority (such as a parent, teacher, trainer or anyone in power). If so, take time to chew on them and ask yourself, 'Is this really true?', 'What personal experience do I have that confirms my world-view?' and 'What might a more liberating belief be?'

Now start aligning your true beliefs and assumptions with your approach to team coaching. Keep making adjustments until your approach is really congruent with who you are.

4 A Team Coaching Journey

> Coaching is all about a journey and nothing about instruction or teaching. It is as much if not more about the way things are done as about what is done.
>
> – SIR JOHN WHITMORE (1992)

The phone rings, you pick up and, out of the blue, an unfamiliar voice says: 'We are looking for a team coach and you come highly recommended. Can we talk?' You reply, 'I have ten minutes right now, how can I help?' The voice says, 'My name is Colin and I am the people director of a challenger bank. I have been asked to find a team coach to support our new leadership team. Can you tell me a bit about your approach?'

What do you say? Perhaps you respond in true coaching style, with a question: 'Before I do, can you tell me more about the team and what they want to achieve?' You're off to a good start; you listen until Colin pauses. You thank him for the information and summarise what you heard, then ask: 'What does team coaching mean to you?' followed by a series of other questions including 'Why now?' And 'Why me?' Eventually you realise the ten minutes is over and you haven't told Colin a jot about you or your approach.

If this sounds like a trap you could get caught in, you are not alone. Listening, summarising and asking questions is in our DNA as coaches. Conversely, being the subject of the conversation means being in the spotlight, and coaches are adept at turning the torch quickly back on others! While learning more about the team and the organisation are essential, Colin wants to know about you and your approach, so you need to be prepared to articulate this clearly.

These days, many leaders have experienced one-to-one coaching. Many organisations who sponsor executive coaching know what a coaching programme looks like. Some even prescribe an approach and expect leaders and their coaches to adopt this. Coaching is a mature profession, and nowadays there is a whole body of knowledge and experience pointing to what good looks like. Team coaching is a much younger discipline, and few coaches really know what it is, so how can potential clients be expected to be clear on what they are expecting or need? We know what we have seen, heard about or experienced and, while many clients will have attended facilitated workshops or team development sessions, most have not experienced *real team coaching*. Also, many trainers, facilitators and consultants have rebadged their work 'team coaching', contributing to the general confusion.

So, rather than expecting prospective clients to be clear on what team coaching is and what great looks like, coaches need to paint a clear picture of what team coaching is. Two key features of this picture are a) your definition of team coaching, translated into the client's language, and b) a visual map of the journey showing the waypoints along the route. This journey map is a 'straw man' serving as an initial proposal which, should you agree to work together, can be refined iteratively with the team. Outlining the different stages of a team coaching programme provides some structure, which many find reassuring. Each stage or phase of the journey has a different focus and intent. Each involves the team in distinct pieces of work, and each requires a shift in the role of the team coach.

> The map appears to us more real than the land.
>
> – D.H. LAWRENCE, 'Study of Thomas Hardy'

It is essential to remember that the 'map is not the territory'; a map or model is an abstraction or implication of reality, and reality itself is a lot messier. Once the journey has begun, all sorts of events are likely to occur that could not have been predicted along the way. Businesses are bought and sold; team members leave and new members join; there are boom economies and recessions; political or legal changes can alter the landscape significantly; and technological advances create new opportunities that were previously not even on the horizon. Think about all the changes you have experienced over any period of 12 months and you'll be amazed. The team coaching journey therefore needs to be agile and adaptive, rather than cast in stone.

A useful first step in designing your own team coaching journey map is to consider how you work with individual coaching clients, if indeed you do. Bring to mind the journey right from initial contact to the very end; what are the distinct phases that you travel through?

Typically, one-to-one coaching programmes cover some or all of these stages, although not necessarily in this order:

➤ *Initial contact:* the first inquiry about coaching.

➤ *Chemistry meeting:* to clarify the brief and establish whether coach and client are a good fit.

➤ *Kick-off meeting:* committing to and scoping the work, and overall contracting on how coach and client will work together.

➤ *Engaging with sponsors:* to gather input and contract around roles and boundaries; mid- and/or endpoint reviews.

➤ *Discovery:* gathering data, psychometric and other assessments, 360° interviews, etc.; observing the client in action.

➤ *Coaching sessions:* working on topics that the client brings in service of the overall coaching agenda.

➤ *Final session:* reviewing learnings, celebrating success, acknowledging unfinished business.

I have intentionally asked you to reflect on your approach before sharing the TCS approach. Why? Because people often abandon what they think in the quest to 'get it right'. No matter how tempting it may be to ignore the wisdom within you, it will serve you well to base your team coaching practice on an approach that you know works for you. Then, looking at other approaches can be a source of inspiration upon which your practice can evolve, rather than putting yours through the shredder.

Mapping the journey

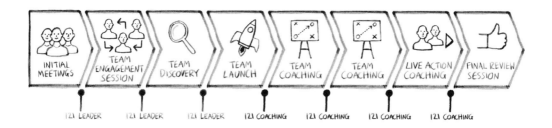

Team coaching journey

Here, I will share with you a typical team coaching journey to illustrate the different phases of work and what each might involve.

As I begin to write about our journey map, I notice some resistance in me. This is partly because I truly believe that there is not one right way to team coach. Also, because it conveys a process that is more systematic and methodical than the messy reality of team coaching. Nonetheless, most team coaching programmes I have delivered involve some or all of these phases.

Now, let's look at each phase in turn.

Initial meetings

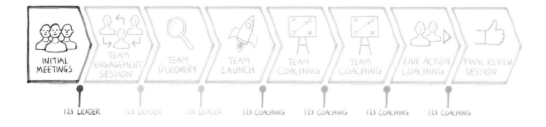

The journey begins with the very first contact, often inviting you to a discussion about a client's team coaching needs. The first few minutes of dialogue about a prospective piece of work can be very illuminating, so pay attention beyond the words to what is potentially being communicated indirectly. What do you notice about the speaker's tone of voice, the pace and sense of urgency? What might be implied around power and who the most 'important' stakeholders are? To what degree are you being wooed or overly flattered? What hoops are you being asked to jump through before any work can be agreed? To what degree do you sense fear, failure, blame or scapegoating?

I recently received a call from a learning and development (L&D) director asking whether I would be available to coach their executive team. She went on to describe a leader who was very experienced in their industry and whose team was under a lot of pressure to perform. She said she would scope out a whole brief with me before I could have an initial conversation with the leader. She then prescribed what my team coaching should look like, including the two-day kick-off which had to happen on dates that were already fixed the following week. I was to start with a call with each team member and then a call with the leader the day before the two-day event to share the results of the interviews. The interviews were really just to get people to meet me, as the coaching programme needed to focus on team members being more accountable and to deliver on their performance goals. The leader would 'drop in' at the start of the two days but would only stay for an hour as he was very busy. In the 15-minute call, the director asked me nothing about myself or my approach.

Even though it was just an initial call, I felt a lot of pressure. I sensed that the L&D director felt a need to protect the leader. I also noted the absence of the leader, in the call and in the proposed programme. I became aware of the caller's need to tightly control the coaching and the prescriptive nature of the relationship, which left me little room to bring my own experience or approach to the table. As the call progressed, I noticed my own drop in energy and lack of appetite for the work.

I declined the work as I was unable to meet their timeline and did not feel that I could add sufficient value working in this way.

You can be more effective as a team coach right from the initial contact by being clear on what you most need to know as it's unlikely you'll have time to cover everything. Here are some useful questions:

Agenda for the call	➤ How long do you both have for the conversation?
	➤ What do you most need from the discussion?
	➤ What do you want to know about me and my approach?
About the team	➤ What team is seeking coaching?
	➤ Who is the leader(s)?
	➤ How many team members are there?
	➤ How long have they been formed?
	➤ What is your relationship with the team?
Learning or change agenda	➤ What learning or change is the team hoping to accomplish through team coaching?
	➤ Why are you/they considering this now?
About me	➤ Why me?
	➤ What brought you to contact me?
About team coaching	➤ What is your/the organisation's/the team's experience of team coaching?
	➤ What does team coaching mean to you?
	➤ What thoughts do you have about what a team coaching programme might look like?
	➤ What is your timeline and budget?
Action	➤ What are the next steps?

There are always more questions that could be asked, but time is inevitably limited. And there is a danger of eliciting more information than you need before you have agreed to take the job. Make sure you leave time to talk about your approach and coaching style as the sponsor is likely to need this to decide whether to put you in touch with the team leader.

First meeting with team leader

Once the commission to coach the team is agreed, you are likely to meet the team leader (if you didn't in the initial call) and perhaps a sponsor. In my experience, there is usually a nominated 'team leader'. However, there is a rise in self-governing teams where leadership is evenly distributed across the team, in which case I would want to meet with the whole team.

This initial meeting with the team leader may well be the first point of contact with someone who is a member of the team to be coached. As in the conversation you had while being recruited for the job, it is important to be clear on your goal, gathering just enough information for the next step and being prepared to share your approach. In addition, my radar tunes into other questions and dynamics, such as:

➤ Does the leader see themselves as a team member, possibly referring to the team as 'us' rather than 'them'? If not, I will need to clarify that a team includes the team's leader and that, for coaching to be effective, it will need their full participation.

➤ Is the leader up for being coached as part of the team coaching? If so, are they willing to be coached with the team present? Being coached can surface vulnerabilities, and some leaders are not willing to take off their armour in front of their team. This does not necessarily prevent the team coaching from being helpful, but it is likely to have greater impact when the process is as transparent as possible. Because I believe that leadership contributes as much as 50 per cent to a team's effectiveness, one of my conditions for taking on a team coaching assignment is that the leader is open for coaching both one-to-one (on how they lead the team) and with the team.

➤ What are the leader's beliefs about their role as team leader? For instance, a leader who sees their role as top-down management could have their authority undermined by a coach whose preference is distributed authority and consensus decision-making. This can often be the case, especially when team coaches haven't unpacked their own personal beliefs and values about leadership.

> ➤ Who will be the primary decision-makers about the team coaching? What will the learning and change agenda be? How will progress will be monitored? And so on. This is a very powerful question, as the nature of the response often reveals a hidden dynamic in the team's system that might be a key to necessary change.

> ➤ Who are the team's primary stakeholders and sponsors? What is their relationship with the team? What are their expectations for the team coaching? What involvement might they have?

For example, I asked a leader of a team of 14 about how decisions were made in the team. She replied that they made decisions collectively. I asked her 'How do you make a decision if you don't all agree?' She replied, 'It's fine, we always reach an agreement.' In an early session in the team, I noticed that, when the time came to decide, all members went quiet and the leader called the decision. No one spoke out, appearing to align with the decision. After the meeting, however, few people acted on the decisions made, resulting in a dynamic where the leader was continually checking progress and challenging the team on their performance, or lack thereof. The leader was privately known as a 'critical parent', always checking up on team members who in turn were disowning their part in decision-making and alignment.

There is so much that you can explore with a team leader, including discovering more about their stakeholders and sponsors and their relationship with the team coaching.

The next step after my initial meeting with the team's leader(s) is usually to meet the team as a whole in a 'team engagement session'.

Team engagement

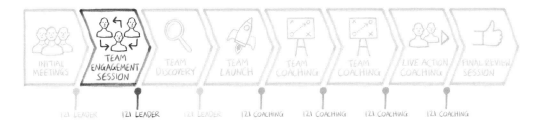

Like a chemistry session that you may have with a potential new client, the purpose of a team engagement session is to meet the team and explore what they want from team coaching and to establish whether you are the right coach for the work. Frequently, I find that many coaches only meet the team for the first time after a programme of team coaching has been agreed. I challenge this approach, as an ethical standard in professional coaching is that coaching is voluntary. If you see the team as your client, then it stands to reason that team members need to meet the coach to understand what they can expect and what will be expected of them. If you are meeting the team for the first time, say for one-to-one interviews as part of a process that they have already been signed up for, this may run counter to the voluntary principle and it could be a tacit indication that you are seeing the team leader as your client and not the team as a whole.

I empathise with concerns that it will take too much time to get the team in the room for an engagement session. What I have found works best is to ask when the team is next meeting and to ask for 60–90 mins of their agenda. I rarely find barriers to this, even in the most powerful and busy teams. The degree to which they make this happen may also be an indication of their appetite for team coaching.

During the engagement session, I encourage you to speak openly and passionately about what it takes for team coaching to be successful. I usually say something along these lines: 'Team coaching can deliver real value and can be one of the best experiences of your career as it is a wonderful feeling to be part of a phenomenally successful team. However, it takes utter commitment to the team and the team coaching process. This means showing up for and engaging fully in team coaching sessions, following up on agreements and actions and having conversations that you may have been avoiding. It will take courage, a sense of responsibility to the team and a hunger for learning.'

One of the side benefits of a team engagement session is the opportunity to observe how the team members engage with each other, to feel the atmosphere of the team and sense any unspoken dynamics, and to assess if there is sufficient appetite and energy in the team for the team coaching.

One of the questions on my mind throughout all the initial meetings and team engagement sessions is whether the team are ready for team coaching. I will come back to this later in this chapter.

 Go to the book website to download an example agenda for a Team Engagement Session.

Team discovery

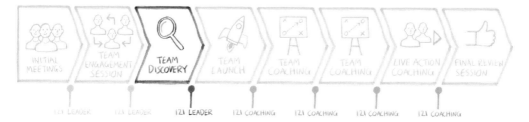

The next phase on the team coaching journey focuses on discovery, the purpose of which is to raise awareness, enabling the team to identify opportunities for learning and change. The team discovery work will therefore influence the design and focus of all subsequent phases of the journey.

As with one-to-one coaching, clients often have a sense that they want something as a result of working with a coach, however unclear they may be as to what this something actually is. They often need us to guide them through a period of exploration to create awareness of their potential. Teams know they can be better, more effective and more cohesive, but often need some insight into what that looks like and some reassurance as to how to get there.

A team discovery phase might include any number of activities designed to heighten the team's awareness and encourage collective responsibility. Some common activities follow.

Team leader interview

Ask the leader more in-depth questions about their beliefs around what makes a good leader and how they see their role. This may enable you to become aware of any concerns or vulnerabilities they might have about executing their role. You can also ask about the team's stakeholders and the quality of stakeholder relationships.

For example, one team leader said to me that he was passionate about the team's vision and the people in their business. He added that he hated conflict and preferred to lead through inspiration. He had one team member that he didn't trust and who continually said what he thought people wanted to hear in meetings and then acted against this outside the room. The leader had not discussed this with the team, fearing confrontation, and had hoped that 'he would come around in time'. One-to-one coaching with the team leader was incredibly helpful in supporting him to find a way to have 'difficult conversations' in a way that was authentic to his leadership style.

Team member interviews

These are usually conducted one-to-one and in a semi-structured form, meaning that all team members are asked the same questions with the option of going 'off piste' if the contributor has particular interests or concerns.

Primary stakeholder interviews

Depending on the purpose and remit of the team coaching, it may be desirable to explore the team's relationship with its stakeholders. As discussed in Chapter 10, most teams have a role to play in the wider organisational system. While there may have been clarity when the team was first assembled, it can easily become disconnected from other teams and from their stakeholders' needs. Team coaching can be instrumental in helping a team to reconnect with its stakeholders, to understand their needs and to clarify the purpose that the team needs to serve.

During our first meeting, I noticed the executive board of a substantial charity talking about 'managing' the chair. I was curious what they meant by 'managing', and they explained that they tried their best to keep the chair at arm's length so that he couldn't interfere. I asked: 'What are the chair's expectations of you as an executive board?' Their response was that the chair had been in post for just six months and was relatively new and therefore still learning about the organisation. I asked the question again; they paused, and then the CEO said: 'To be honest, I don't think I have asked.' In that moment, they became aware of the disconnect and set about a plan to engage more proactively with the chair and trustees.

One way of getting stakeholders' voices into the room is by conducting interviews. I recommend keeping the list of questions short – around five to seven is enough – to allow time for a richer exploration around each. I am sure you can come up with some excellent questions that are context specific to the team you are working with.

There are various ways that this data can be gathered, including coach-led interviews, team-led interviews, HR- or organisational sponsor-led interviews, online questionnaires, and so on. In my view, the most impactful approach is for the team themselves to interview stakeholders and then to make sense of the resulting data together. This increases ownership, and relationships start to strengthen through the process. I tend to find that online 360° questionnaires in this context are the least helpful as the data often requires further dialogue between the team and their stakeholders to clarify understanding, and this could be achieved through quality conversations in the first place.

Stakeholders can also be invited to meet with the team as a whole to discuss what they need from the team. You can also use the 'empty chair' technique described in Chapter 12. Ultimately, the value of stakeholder data is to shape the team's purpose, their *big why*.

In a fast-growth digi-tech organisation, conflict was escalating between the marketing and products teams. The marketing director told me 'We are a marketing-led organisation' and proceeded to say that the products team were the problem: they were working to their own set of priorities and they frequently missed deadlines. His view was that the marketing team was being let down by the products team. During the discovery phase of their team coaching programme, members of the marketing team set about doing their own 'market research' whereby pairs of team members interviewed different stakeholder groups. They were surprised at what came back. The executive team said that a road map of products and timelines was agreed quarterly in an executive team meeting, and the marketing team needed to line up their campaigns to support the roll-out of products. The IT and sales teams both saw the marketing team as arrogant and 'acting like they were running the whole show'. The CEO helped make sense of the confusion, explaining that marketing had led a massively successful advertising campaign several years ago. Indeed, it was so successful that the cartoon characters in the adverts were famous, and this had directly increased brand awareness and customer loyalty. In celebration, the CEO had said they were a 'marketing-led' organisation, but they had never unpacked what this meant. Through dialogue, the marketing team reconfigured the team's purpose in consultation with their stakeholders as 'To let the world know about the brilliance of our products and to delight our customers'.

Team assessments

When I first started team coaching, as part of my approach I tried using psychometric assessments such as personality and conflict indicators, emotional intelligence tools, surveys on drivers and satisfaction, and various reports on individual strengths. In general, teams found this useful for getting to know one another better. These tools often encourage an understanding of individual preferences and differences which can improve communication. However, they lacked real impact on the team's everyday collaboration. One day it dawned on me that I was focusing the team on the *individual in the system* rather than focusing on the team *as a system*. In other words, I was encouraging the team to pay attention to the dancers rather than the dance.

An effective team is more than the sum of its parts, and teams don't become effective by working on the parts – they do this by working on the whole.

At the time, the same assessment providers started to produce 'team reports', which they did by aggregating the results. This approach has two flaws:

1. With a team, the whole is more than the sum of the parts. You get the horsepower of each team member when you focus on the parts. The horsepower of the team is leveraged when the collective effort is channelled effectively in one direction, towards the team's purpose.

2. An average or aggregated team score ignores the power dynamics in the team. An influential team member or subgroup, a dominant leader or a particularly compelling organisational culture will skew a team's profile and preferences; however, this does not show up on reports where member scores are averaged.

With this in mind, we encourage the use of assessments which measure the team as a system, for example the Team Diagnostic Survey (TDS) and teamSalient.

Team Diagnostic Survey

The TDS is based on research conducted by Harvard's Wageman, Hackman and Lehman on the conditions that foster team effectiveness. The report shows the team's scores on '6 Team Conditions' and demonstrates how these contribute to team effectiveness. There are three *essential* conditions: compelling purpose, real team and right people; and three *enabling* ones: sound structure, supportive context and, you will be glad to know, team coaching.

They see the role of leadership as creating and maintaining the conditions. The TDS therefore provides leaders and teams with incredibly useful insight into how well their team is designed and set up for success, and potential improvements that can be made.

Their research, published in *Senior Leadership Teams: What It Takes to Make Them Great* (Wageman et al., 2008), has profoundly influenced my practice as a team coach. Check out their website at **www.6teamconditions.com** and their podcasts, blogs and articles.

When appropriate, I tend to use TDS at the beginning of a team coaching programme to explore the team's structure and design, as good foundations enable my team coaching to have greater impact.

teamSalient

A diagnostic tool designed to measure a team's effectiveness across its different stages of development, teamSalient was developed by my colleague Dr Declan Woods. It was co-designed with teams, for teams, and draws upon quantitative scientific research over several years with extensive field testing in over 200 teams.

The tool measures the whole team in context: its structure, processes, group dynamics and team member relationships, and compares this with other teams. It measures a team's success against 16 drivers of team effectiveness (e.g. team glue or psychological safety) and identifies which ones have the greatest bearing on results, bringing focus to the team's development. In-built action plans allow a team to track progress as it develops over time.

teamSalient emphasises the team's leadership and its inter- and intra-team dynamics and how effectively a team works together. I tend to use this assessment with teams after the team design and structure has been established and when the team have experience of working together. See **www.teamsalient.com** for more information.

Team Selfie

Designed by TCS faculty member Allard de Jong, Team Selfie comprises 144 questions divided into six categories: vision and direction; leadership; roles and responsibilities; process/structure/ resources; communication; relationships and system. It is a highly flexible and adaptable tool allowing coaches to tailor the questions with their clients to suit their organisation and situation.

Team Selfie is one of my favourite tools as it invites clients to work co-creatively with the coach in the design of the questionnaire, which in turn increases ownership of the resulting data. It is fantastic as a before-and-after assessment, providing a measure of the progress that the team has made through working with you as their coach.

There are an increasing number of team assessment tools available, and these are just three examples. Rather than a stock approach wheeled out for every client, we recommend selecting and designing the approach with the team collaboratively. Where you can, work with the team or organisation's frame of reference rather than imposing your own tools.

 Visit the book website for example team discovery tools, including interview questions and a free downloadable copy of Team Selfie for your personal use in working with teams.

Team launch

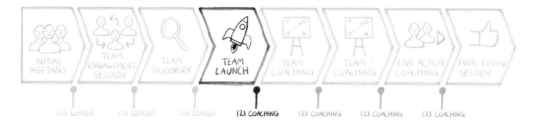

The next stage of our journey is the team launch, where the focus is on forming the team and setting them up for success. This phase often includes elements that support people in getting to know one another better, creating or reviewing a team charter and agreeing team development goals.

The beauty of a team launch is that it brings the team together in a safe, reflective space to experience themselves as a team. This is sometimes designed as a two-day session with an overnight stay, providing team members with social time where they are able to share personal stories and begin to form bonds. However, with the increase of virtual team coaching, this can take the form of iterative sessions spread across a few days or even a week. The launch needs all team members to be present as they will be creating both a practical and psychological contract together that everyone must sign up to.

Many teams prefer to hold this meeting away from their normal place of work to create a sense of space and unity. As team coach, I urge you against designing and facilitating the whole session yourself. It is far better to co-create the experience with the team and to engage different team members in facilitating sessions as this increases awareness and responsibility and distributes leadership.

If the team has opted to use any personality or behavioural assessments, this can be a good time to share and explore the meaning for individuals and implications for the team. They can also begin to explore how team members' strengths can be used in service of the team's purpose and goals. For example, one member of an executive team may be very customer focused, bringing the 'voice of the customer' into the conversation. Another may be a capable scribe, capturing outputs and agreements and tracking progress.

The dialogue and exchange involved in working through the elements of a team charter is invaluable, so make sure the process isn't hurried and that sufficient time is allowed. Too often I have seen the team spend a whole day or more on debriefing assessments and other activities that focus on the individuals in the team and then race through the charter on day two. The format of team charters varies from team to team, and it can take many forms. Typical components include:

➤ *Team purpose:* Why does the team exist? What work does the team do? What role does the team play in the organisation?

➤ *Stakeholders:* Who is the team accountable to? With what other teams do we connect? What do they need from us?

➤ *Key goals:* What specific results do we need to achieve, by when?

➤ *Membership:* Who is on the team? What are their functional roles? What role does each member play for the team?

➤ *Values:* What is important to us as a team? What standards will we live by?

➤ *Working agreements:* What do we expect of each other? How will we make decisions? How will we hold each other to account? How will we handle conflict?

Once the work of creating the team charter is done, I recommend that you coach the team on how they will ensure that it acts as a living guide to the team's focus and working practices. A team charter that is captured in PowerPoint and filed in a shared folder will do little to act as a guide. It is only through discipline that the team will use the team charter as a committed agreement to teamwork.

The team launch can also be used to explore and agree the team's learning or development goals as these are likely to form the focus for the subsequent team coaching. Coaches approach this in many ways; however, the most common is to engage the team in sharing the data gathered during the discovery phase and using this to illuminate the team's learning and change agenda.

Again, I encourage you to co-create with the team how they will process and make use of the data. The more involved the team is in agreeing the approach and managing themselves, rather than simply being facilitated through a pre-designed approach, the more the team will take ownership and responsibility.

One dilemma when using interview data is whether you, the coach, organise the data into themes to turn it into useful insights. While I appreciate the intent, by doing this you are then theming the data by your own frame of reference, rather than inviting the team to do the meaning-making. Also, you may not be identifying the most valuable insights for the team, which could be revealed by a single comment rather than a theme. Instead, I recommend that the team engages in the process of mining the data for gems.

A final note: the team coaching journey model provides a useful visual to the various phases of a team coaching programme. However, some teams will already be well launched, so this phase may not be needed.

 Visit the book website for an example team charter, and other useful tools for a team launch.

Team coaching

Now we are moving on to the fascinating and much more demanding work of actual team coaching. As with one-to-one coaching, team coaching sessions take place on a regular basis, often four to six weeks apart, ranging from a couple of hours to a full day. Sometimes sessions will be more frequent due to the urgency of the team's needs and situation, like in the build-up to the sale of the business or another major transition point.

The focus for the team coaching sessions is likely to be in these areas:

➤ team development goals, as identified in the team launch

➤ embedding the team charter

➤ working through any dynamics which emerge and are impeding the team's progress

➤ horizon-scanning and developing team reflexivity and agility

➤ celebrating successes and integrating lessons learned along the way.

One of the challenges for the team coach is how to arrive at agreed topics for team coaching sessions. This is actually a microcosm of a larger ongoing team process of agreeing and maintaining the team's priorities and focus. It seems that many coaches determine the topics themselves: 'Today we are going to work on reviewing how effectively you are following through on your team charter.' This can avoid the uncertainty and discomfort of team members having different views on the most pressing topic, but it robs the team of the opportunity to learn and hone how they go from 'many to one', a process they will need time and time again to work effectively as a team. So, my preference is to coach the team to decide what process they will use to identify and agree coaching topics instead of providing them with a process to follow or facilitating them. This will initially take longer than if prescribed by the coach; however, it is a great example of 'slowing down to speed up'.

Live action coaching

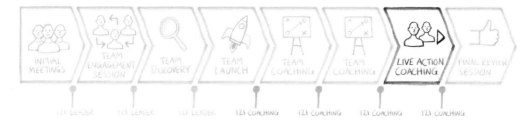

In contrast to team coaching, where the team is engaged in a coaching session focused on a specific topic, live action coaching is about coaching the team while they go about their 'normal work'. It ideally takes place at their usual meeting place, at their usual time. The coach does not facilitate or lead the meeting in any way; instead, he or she is 'off the pitch' while the team in is play. The coach's role is contracted for before the meeting and may include observing:

➤ to what degree members are sticking to their values and working agreements

➤ how effective they are in discussing, debating and making decisions

➤ whether they check for alignment when making decisions

➤ how they hold each other to account

➤ how they keep the needs and expectations of stakeholders in mind

➤ what the atmosphere is like that they are creating

➤ how you are impacted by the team and your 'felt sense'.

Contract clearly with the team around what exactly you are noticing and when and how this will be shared. Can you interrupt the meeting to intervene, or will there be scheduled pauses for reflection and input? Or will you share what you have noticed at the end of the session? Clearly, waiting until the end is the least desirable option as the team will need to remember to apply any behavioural changes or actions in future meetings. However, sometimes teams have guests attending meetings, and they are unlikely to be directly involved in the team coaching.

Live action coaching can be demanding and invigorating as it reveals the nitty-gritty of the team in action. You are no longer with the team discussing how they will work together in the future; it is live and in the here-and-now and is the fount of transformational change.

Individual coaching

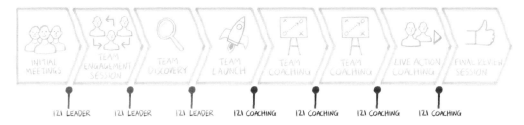

I often get asked in seminars and workshops for my perspective on whether team coaches should offer individual coaching as part of a team coaching programme. I always respond with 'It depends'. Some authors on the subject advocate strongly against offering to coach individual team members, saying the coach should focus on the team as an entity rather than on individuals in the team. They express a concern that coaches will experience a phenomenon called *triangulation* (see Chapter 10), where the coach becomes the recipient of the team's most difficult dynamics and that, rather than address concerns directly with each other, they will attempt to turn the coach into a messenger, delivering information on their behalf.

I understand this concern, but I think this perspective is too black and white. When supervising team coaching, these questions often arise for me:

➤ What is the purpose for the individual coaching?

➤ What boundaries need to be established?

➤ How will boundaries be maintained?

➤ What rules of engagement need to be agreed?

➤ To what degree do you personally have the psychological and diary capacity for both individual and team coaching?

All of the above is subjective and will be informed by your team coaching methodology and approach, as well as by your skills, maturity and capacity as a team coach. We are all different and, while I am not saying you should coach individual team members, I am also not advocating against it either. If individual coaching has a clear purpose, if you can establish an effective team coaching contract, set and maintain clear boundaries, manage yourself and others around any pressure to scapegoat or collude, and you have the bandwidth to cope with the relational load, then go for it!

My own learnings that now inform my practice are these:

1. Ensure that the purpose of any individual coaching is in service of the overall team coaching contract and being more effective as a team.

2. Establish a confidentiality boundary around the team, rather than around individuals. This means that anything shared one-to-one is 'open' to the team coaching. In reality, I encourage team members to discuss any issues they have with another team member directly. I might also offer to help them prepare by rehearsing the conversation. However, if the tension is acted out further, then I would encourage them to work through their differences in the room, with the team as support to the process. In my view, any tension in a team needs to be owned by the team rather than being made to be about style or personality differences between two members.

3. I either coach all individual team members or none. I once made the mistake of agreeing to coach all but one member, who already had a coach. This set up a dynamic where I had an underdeveloped relationship with the one team member, which fed into his lack of engagement in the team coaching.

Final review

The purpose of the final review session is to celebrate success, to integrate learning and to close off the project or business cycle and set the stage for what is to come.

The coach's role here is to support the team in taking full ownership of the discussion, the process, the atmosphere and the experience together. In this way, you avoid the numbing experience of a team simply going through the motions, and the team fully claims and invests in the learning.

It is often tempting to skip or rush through, often because the team's attention is on to 'what next' rather than integrating the learning. It is so often the case in organisational life that people and teams race from one task to the next. However, the final review is a critical phase as it builds capability for the future and it encourages a cycle of continuous learning and growth.

Go/no-go

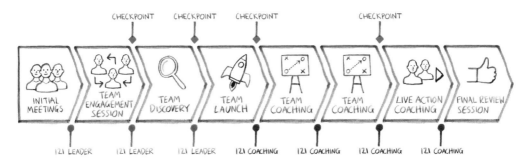

Rather than proposing a full team coaching programme to a potential new client, I factor in several 'go/no-go' checkpoints. These allow us to mutually commit to each stage of the team coaching, at which point we can assess whether there is sufficient value to be gained and appetite for the work.

I adopted the go/no-go checkpoints, as usual, by learning the hard way. In the past I found myself embarking on coaching programmes scheduled over a year, only to discover that the team was not sufficiently committed to the work. This happened either because they had been told they were going to do team coaching and some members went along for the ride, or because various crises kept demanding the attention of the team, so the timing wasn't right. It is also possible that a team will not come to a shared view of the areas of focus for the team coaching or be aligned around the value.

Go/no-go checkpoints allow each party to respectfully withdraw. Often the work done up to the checkpoint is useful; however, there may not be enough energy to sustain further work.

Team Coaching Readiness

By failing to prepare, you are preparing to fail.

– ANON

A programme of team coaching requires considerable time and effort from everyone, including you. It is therefore worth spending the time to assess whether the team is ready for coaching. Ruth Wageman, co-creator of the six conditions for team effectiveness discussed earlier, sometimes uses the metaphor of a farmer who has the best possible seeds for the crop intended. However, if the farmer does not prepare the soil well enough for the crop and maintain the conditions for growth with nutrients, water, sunlight and so on, there is little likelihood of a bumper crop.

The six conditions framework is described in more detail in Chapter 12; it offers one way of assessing team coaching readiness by inviting the team to consider whether the conditions are in place and, if not, to take action to prepare the ground. You can also use checklist-style assessments; you can find examples of these in Chapter 12 and on the website.

An important gauge is how motivated the leader and team members are to engage in team coaching. Without sufficient 'fuel in the tank', the coaching is unlikely to last the duration. It is also valuable to find out whether there is sufficient support from the team's sponsors (such as the team leader's boss, the executive team, HR or budget holder) for the coaching, otherwise the plug could be pulled at any point.

Clearly it is ideal to assess a team's readiness for coaching at the outset. However, sufficient data may not emerge until you are into or through the discovery phase. You may find the need to reassess when you are well into a programme as situations change. Team members or even team leaders may leave the team, new members join, the organisation restructures, a crisis occurs which needs the team's focus and time, the business is acquired or floated – to name but a few unforeseen contingencies.

Reflection time

This chapter covers many tangible and practical elements of team coaching – for a team and coach alike. There are many options and choices for you to inform and differentiate your practice, all of which can benefit from careful consideration. The reflective practice questions here build upon the questions in the previous chapter, so you may wish to remind yourself of your responses to them before engaging with the questions below.

You could start by thinking about your one-to-one coaching. Ask yourself:

➤ How might your approach to one-to-one coaching inform your team coaching offering? What is the same or similar? What is different?

➤ Now think about your team coaching practice. Ask yourself:

➤ What will you carry forward from your one-to-one coaching into your work with teams?

➤ What is your definition of team coaching?

➤ How will you articulate your approach to team coaching to a client? What will you say?

➤ What does the journey look like through team coaching? What is your journey map?

➤ How will a team experience this journey? (This could be particularly important if a team has not undertaken team coaching before.)

➤ What is unique or different about your approach?

➤ Which parts of your team coaching journey are fixed, and which are fluid, i.e., which are critical and will always form part of your approach and which are optional? Which elements of your approach are you willing to be flexible about while remaining congruent to your philosophy and beliefs? Who decides – you as team coach or the team?

➤ Is your approach to discovery more diagnostic or dialogic (conversational)?

➤ Is one-to-one coaching part of your team coaching journey? Will you conduct any one-to-one coaching, or do you consider that presents a conflict of interests? If so, will you refer this work to another coach?

➤ Are the team and/or team's leader ready for team coaching? How do you know?

➤ Are you ready to coach the team?

Your answers to these questions are a vital part of contracting with clients. What is a client asking for and does it match what you are willing and able to offer? If you are not clear on what your team coaching 'offer' is, it is all too easy to be persuaded by a client to take on work that doesn't match your approach or skills or does not meet their needs. Reflect more deeply on:

➤ What are your conditions for successful team coaching?

➤ What are the 'must have' elements for the team coaching to be successful?

➤ What do you need to be present to coach a team successfully? What might this depend upon and what might need to be negotiated with a team and be put into place before or during the coaching?

5 Metaskills: A Process for Change

Between stimulus and response there is a space. In that space is our power to choose our response. In our response lies our growth and our freedom.

– STEPHEN R. COVEY, *First Things First* (inspired by Viktor E. Frankl)

TCS Team Coaching Wheel

The TCS Team Coaching Wheel was designed to provide a compass for coaches, acting as a guide to the mindset, skills and competencies necessary for team coaching excellence. Philosophy and stance sit at the core of the TCS Team Coaching Wheel. Radiating out from the centre are bands of skills and competencies required in team coaching. The band closest to the core contains the *metaskills*: higher-order skills that are essential for impactful team coaching. Surrounding the metaskills are five clusters of team coaching competencies. The outer layer represents the tools, techniques, models and frameworks that you use in your work. This is an inside-out model, as we believe that the quality of your work depends on your own interior condition. So, it's not what you are doing or how you are doing it, it's the source that you are operating from. In this part of the book, I will dive more deeply into the metaskills with the aim of bringing them to life for you.

What are metaskills?

> Metaskills... are inherent in any person who has a Taoist orientation to life; that is, anyone interested in following the ebb and flow of nature.
>
> – MINDELL (1995)

Metaskills are higher-order skills that supercharge every aspect of team coaching. Originating from the Greek word *meta*, meaning 'after' or 'beyond', metaskills transcend all other skills. Metaskills can be cultivated over time, shaping your practice. To the beginner, metaskills can seem mechanical. Gradually, they will freely and easily become part of your own distinctive style.

The three metaskills of *presence*, *use of self* and *active experiments* are essential for creating awareness, choice and experimentation. Together they provide team coaches with a powerful methodology for change. They are woven together, each reliant upon and energised by the others.

Presence

The coach with little awareness of their presence and its impact is operating partially blind. The coach who has yet to learn how to use different aspects of self is not yet that finely tuned instrument of influence and change.

– BLUCKERT (2015)

Your 'presence' is your distinctive way of being – and how you bring coaching skills to life. The skills, tools and techniques you gather along the way are your equipment; the unique way you apply them is coloured by your presence. Imagine a room full of portrait artists in a studio painting a live model. Imagine they are working with the same paper, identical sets of brushes and the same colour palette. Despite the conditions being indistinguishable, each picture will be utterly unique. This happens without them trying to be different; they are simply using their own way. Fritz Perls and Dick Price were two gestalt therapists. They used the same methodology, yet Price was passive and gentle while Perls was directive and provocative.

Your presence may be invisible to you yet marvelled at by others. Most of us have limited awareness of our presence and the impact it has on clients. Your signature presence can perhaps be thought of as your *default style*, the 'natural you' before tools and skills are added. No matter how hard you try to mimic someone you admire, or to fit with a certain norm, you will invariably revert back to your default. This is good news, as this is a crucial part of what you bring to your work. It is here that you are likely to feel in flow and experience a deep sense of congruence between your work and your self.

Presence is as inescapable as it is inevitable because you bring yourself into any coaching relationship. Even if you try to minimise yourself as much as you humanly can, you still have a presence – you cannot be neutral even if you would like to be.

> Everyone possesses presence, regardless of the level of awareness of the impact of that presence.
>
> – NEVIS (1992)

But presence is not the same as charisma, which is about charm, power and persuasiveness – an outer image that can be 'put on' or worn like a cloak. Presence is more visceral and intuitive, emanating from deep within us. It is your way of being in the world, imbued with all your unique history, the culture you are part of, your education, your family, your lived experiences, your fears, your judgements and your biases. It is infused by the future – your hopes and dreams for your life and the difference you want to make in the world.

Presence can attract, fascinate, energise and influence others. It can also repel, alienate, drain and discourage others too. Your presence is in your typical patterns of relating and what this tends to evoke in others. Take your whole life history and throw this into the mix with all your training and practical life experience and the result is *you* as team coach – the integrated totality of all you have become.

Simply, presence is how *you* do *you*.

The flow of attention

> Flow is being completely involved in an activity for its own sake. The ego falls away. Time flies. Every action, movement and thought follows inevitably from the previous one, like playing jazz.
>
> – Mihaly Csikszentmihalyi, 'Go with the Flow', *Wired* (1996)

Presence also encompasses your ability to be present and in flow. When you are fully in the moment, you can respond to the team, to the situation that you are in and to what you become aware of in yourself. A delightfully simple yet powerful model is STS, which stands for Self, Team and Situation. Being effective as team coaches requires us to be fully present to each of the three elements, flowing our attention between them.

STS: the flow of attention
Adapted from the SOS model, Denham-Vaughan & Chidiac (2013)

Self: You are grounded and centred and present to yourself. You are aware of your thoughts, feelings and sensations. You are aware of shifts in energy and how the team is affecting you. For example, you notice a tightening in your stomach as a team member makes a comment that lands like a bomb two minutes before the end of a session.

Team: You are connected with the team and team members. You are aware of and responding to the thoughts, feelings and needs of each person and the team as a whole. For example, rising frustration is apparent as conflict escalates between two team members.

Situation: You are aware of the team's wider context, the time available and the task in hand. You are noticing what is happening in any given moment, such as a team struggling to reach agreement on a major decision that is key to their presentation to the board the following day.

All three elements are embedded within a given context and culture, which have a strong influence on what is possible and how, as a coach, you respond.

Each of us has an awareness bias, meaning that our attention naturally is more on one of the three elements. Successful team coaching requires that you flow your attention across all three interrelated elements, finding a balance between them.

Martha became aware that her attention was often on herself. Her inner dialogue was focused on how well she was performing as a coach and whether she looked good. Her attention then flowed to the situation, wanting to make sure the tasks were done well and on time, as this was connected to her own need to perform. Her attention rested less on individuals or the team as a whole. Together this created a pattern in her work of disconnecting people or the team. Missing when they needed to stay with a conversation that had emerged, she would cut through, saying 'you have two minutes left' to complete the task or arrive at a decision. Her learning edge was to become more present to all three domains by consciously flowing her attention between them.

Presence demands confidence. Like a martial arts black belt who can centre and ground themselves before making a clear and intentional move; you are present to yourself, the team and the situation, even during the heat of strong emotions or conflict. You can self-manage and are not overpowered by or enmeshed in the team's emotions and dynamics, maintaining your presence under pressure. This doesn't mean being poker-faced either; indeed, quite the opposite – it means being fully open to 'STS', responding to moments as they arise.

Developing your presence

Presence is a far more potent variable than tools or techniques, allowing the coach to respond to the moments of uncertainty with distinctive impact and transparency that inspires others.

– SIMINOVITCH & VAN ERON (2008)

Presence is illusive. It requires you to become aware of the many facets of your self. Examine your own beliefs, judgements, values, feelings, reactions and motives, and ask yourself how these may be impacting your work.

When working with clients, I am often told that I am very calm and grounded and that this creates a sense of safety and ease. People tell me that they feel able to be themselves and to speak up when I am holding the space. This enables me to do work that other coaches might prefer not to do.

What is the impact of your style on your life and work? What is it about you and your way of being that has an effect? If you don't have a sense of this, I encourage you to find out.

So far, I have asked you to think about the things that make your presence unique. I now invite you to dig deeper to discover the many shades of the palette of your presence.

Some of the elements of presence are your personal history, the culture or cultures you grew up in and the one(s) you are now part of. Also, your education and the gifts and talents that you discovered. Relationships that have influenced you and your way of being, along with life experiences and how you dealt with them, are also part of this.

As we have seen, your presence can be thought of as your default style, but in reality, you don't have just one defining way of being. Behind your default, you have other aspects of your presence that may be more hidden or out of your awareness. We all habituate a favoured way of being, especially if this is mostly effective in our work. But you are multidimensional, and you have a range of ways of being that you can draw on. When you don't have access to your full range, your identity becomes fixed or rigid and you limit the range of responses available to you, thereby limiting the impact you can have. Mastery lies in accessing your range.

For example, if you see yourself as a calm person, then you may remain calm in all situations, whereas a well-developed range might include the ability to be animated. If you see yourself as an active or dynamic person, can you also slow right down?

Anna has a default presence that is very empathetic and attentive. She is very warm and connects easily with people. However, when working with groups, she can easily get exhausted as she works hard to make each person feel fully met and attended to, often absorbing the tensions and dynamics in the group. She feels she can 'breathe again' once harmony is restored. The impact of Anna's natural presence is that she creates safety and builds trust and intimacy with people. However, her way of being was so automatic that she had no control over it, even when the situation required her to be different.

Anna's stretch was to establish greater range. In supervision, I invited her to identify what the polarity of her default presence might be. She decided it was more detached and more connected to herself than to others. Gradually, by deliberately extending her range, she developed a conscious ability to pull back and to reconnect with herself. She noticed that this had an impact on the team she was coaching, in that as she pulled back in this way, team members started to lean in, attending to each other more, rather than relying on her to do so.

The opposite pole of your default presence can also be thought of as your shadow self. We all made childhood decisions about how we must and mustn't be: 'I must be kind and generous' or 'Never blow your own trumpet' or 'Man up'. Known as introjects, these become part of our script, the operating system that guides our thoughts and actions. Embracing your shadow can be challenging but also massively liberating, and as you grow, your effectiveness as a team coach grows too.

I embrace my shadow self. Shadows give depth and dimension to my life. I believe in embracing my duality, in learning to let darkness and light, peacefully co-exist, as illumination.

– JAEDA DEWALT

A highly intelligent and analytical man, Oscar was known for his quick thinking and agile mind. He could take in vast amounts of data from disparate sources and then state the essence or core theme in a few words. This was magical to behold, and I relished moments when this happened. I worked with Oscar often over a few years and became familiar with another aspect of his presence. When in this mode, he would often stand up wearing a mischievous expression and invite the team to do something playful, quite out of the blue! Never once did a team turn down his invitation. There was something about the serious credibility of his primary presence that enabled people to also shift to letting go and having fun when he went there himself.

A helpful way to think about presence is *the capacity to be present to all that is*. Be present to the many dimensions of yourself, including your shadow and the aspects you may have disowned. Be present to the same in others, recognising we all have shadows that often mask other strengths and possibilities. Grow your capacity to be present to all situations as they arise, sitting in the fire. Be present to the context and culture that the team is located within. To be present to all that is, without becoming consumed by it, requires that your attention flows rather than fixates on one aspect of the field.

The purpose is to understand your presence and what it evokes in others, so that you can use it intentionally.

Evocative and provocative presence

Our state of being is the only real source of our ability to influence the world.

– GARDNER (1984)

Fundamentally, the aim of the use of self is to evoke awareness and provoke action by intervening in the most powerful way possible. Nevis (1992) explains, 'The practitioner is not only to stand for and express certain values, attitudes and skills, but to use these in a way to stimulate, and perhaps evoke from the client, action necessary for movement on its problems.'

Mastery as a team coach derives from flowing your attention between the team, the situation and yourself (STS) and, in response to what is emerging, intentionally shifting between an evocative presence and a provocative presence to maximise the impact of your interventions.

Self as 'evocateur' is a highly effective mode for raising awareness as it helps the team to assess the situation, give rise to understanding and generate options. The team is still exploring, and the agenda is still emerging. You embody an *evocative* presence, holding the space and inviting listening, curiosity and genuine responding. This is a soft, gentle, holding presence that builds trust and the safety necessary for risk-taking and self-disclosure. When being an evocative presence, you are not inviting action; you are using your presence to give voice to what is 'in the room'; naming that which is often implicit, lying unspoken until now. This brings shape to the team's collective thoughts and feelings and supports collective meaning-making.

While being an evocative presence, you can also track the collective energy of the team. I often imagine an ocean; I am looking for enough energy to rise up from under the surface to create a wave. With teams, there needs to be enough collective energy to mobilise into action. An experienced coach can feel the energy rising; once it does, they shift into a *provocative* presence, challenging the team to move into action.

Self as provocateur is an action-orientated and bold intervention style with the aim of provoking change. Saying to a team that their behaviour is inconsistent with their desire to act as one team is provocative. Provocative interventions can spark a range of responses, from surprise to excitement, or from slight irritation to infuriation. To make good use of the spark of energy, you can then engage the team in an active experiment, inviting them to try something new.

Using a provocative presence means taking risks and being opportunistic. Your intent is to stir things up, but not to start a riot. To this aim, grade your interventions using your experience of the team, your trust in yourself and the process to dial your provocative presence up or down. When being a provocative presence, you are 'dancing' on the edge between certainty and uncertainty, not knowing how the team might respond. Change takes place at the boundary of what is known or habitual and something different. Team coaches work at the boundary, using an evocative presence to maintain the relationship and shifting into a provocative presence to disturb it and invite change.

Use of Self

> Presence is the integrated totality of what we have developed and worked to become; use of self is how one leverages one's presence to impact and to strategically provoke client work.
>
> – SIMINOVITCH, 2017

Presence is all that you bring to the here-and-now moment; use of self is responding to what is happening in the moment – it is presence in action.

I am writing about presence and use of self here as though they are distinct competencies, yet in reality they are inseparable. The tango is a wonderfully dramatic and emotional dance. There are steps and rules to be followed, but the movement of the dancers is personal in its dynamics and expression. The passion and emotion that each dancer feels is conveyed through the steps. It is the expression of connection between dance partners, the music and the unique moment, rather than about the choreography. Whereas the tango is a feeling that is danced, use of self is a feeling that is expressed.

Imagine that you are working with a team. You are fully present and in the moment rather than thinking about what is next or what just happened. You are engaged in and attending to what is going on right now. You are aware, noticing and tuned in to yourself and the group. After a while of observing with 'soft eyes', you have a clear figure of interest – an interactional pattern, an image, a feeling, a sensation, an intuition. You choose to respond and 'make a move'. You intervene. You put into words what you are experiencing with the team.

This is the moment when awareness from your presence becomes 'use of self'. It is the way that you act upon what you are noticing in order to have an effect on the team and their situation.

Where presence is being, use of self is doing.

In reality, you are 'using your self' all the time in every relationship and situation – you just may not be doing it intentionally. Recently, I watched a movie about a young mother who becomes the target of road rage. In one terrifying scene after another, she is aggressively pursued by a broken and distressed man who has nothing left to lose. As the pressure mounted, I found the tension almost unbearable. I could feel my heart pounding, and I realised I had been sitting with my hand covering my mouth, no doubt in a wide-eyed stare. This is a rather dramatic example of the fact that people are impacting each other all the time. Yet we are so used to numbing our feelings that we often don't notice unless a high-stakes drama is playing out. So, practise tuning in and noticing the impact that people, teams and everyday experiences are having on you.

As team coaches, use of self is at the heart of our work.

A skilful team coach tunes in to a team's atmosphere and establishes a presence that supports its psychological safety, evokes awareness and provokes experimentation and change. The goal of any coaching intervention is to raise the team's awareness around a shared 'figure of interest' – a particular topic, dynamic, pattern or situation. Earlier, we looked at the flow of attention (STS) where you become aware of, and flow your attention between, *self*, *team* and the *situation*. These three elements of awareness assist teams in understanding their experience, creating meaning and generating new possibilities and choices. Once awareness has been sufficiently raised, then the work is to get into action as this is how change is brought about.

To intervene powerfully, you:

➤ flow your attention across self, team and the situation (STS)

➤ expand the range of your presence, from evocative to provocative

➤ shift intentionally between the three team coaching 'modes'.

Now let's take a look at these modes.

The three modes of team coaching

A 'mode' is the manner in which something is experienced, expressed or done. When you are working as a team coach, you switch between these modes with clear intent.

Three modes of team coaching

Looking at this illustration, the first thing to notice is that the team, the coach (in mode 1) and their task are inside a circle. In this space, all three entities are 'on the pitch' in direct relationship with each other. Mode 1 is about using yourself as a facilitator, by holding the space, asking questions and offering tools and exercises. Like a traffic cop, you are directing the flow of the traffic. You are leading or directing the process while the team engages in a task or activity.

Examples of mode 1 in action are:

1. Setting up an activity, such as inviting the team to split into subgroups and discuss a specific subject. Here, you are focusing the team's attention and providing procedural instructions for the activity in hand. You are also holding the space, managing the activity against the available time, answering questions and offering clarifying information.

2. Sitting in the round, you pose a question or topic to the team and invite each member to speak. Their replies are mostly to you. Here, you are directing the team's focus, and choreographing the conversation.

3. In plenary, the team is seated, and you are standing at the flipchart and capturing responses. Here you are in a position of power – standing while team members are sitting – holding the flipchart pens, scribing. Their attention is on you and the flipchart.

In mode 2, you metaphorically 'helicopter' up in order to observe the team's interactional patterns. The team are in discussion or immersed in an activity. You are noticing. Who passes to whom and how often? Who leads, who follows? Where are clusters or subgroups forming?

Another way of thinking about this is to imagine you are on a theatre balcony, watching the dance. The sense of being high up above the team means that your focus is more directed to patterns than on the content of what people are saying or what individual team members are doing. You are observing the dance and how the performers are in motion together.

In mode 2, you notice and selectively offer observations on the team's interactional patterns. Examples of this mode in action are:

1. You observe that two members have been in dialogue for quite some time, with the rest of the team seemingly disconnected from the conversation, looking away or fiddling with their mobile phones. You intervene: 'I notice that David and Sian have been talking between themselves for the last five minutes. I'm curious where others are on this subject.' How you communicate this makes all the difference. Seek to find a tone and body language that is curious and non-judgemental.

2. You observe that the conversation is going around in circles and, rather than building on each other's ideas with the intent of reaching a decision, team members are going off at tangents. A metaphor comes to mind, and you intervene: 'I notice an image comes to mind of an octopus, and each leg trying to swim in a different direction. What might this mean for you?'

3. You observe that one team member is repeatedly late or missing from team sessions and no one has mentioned it. You say, 'I notice Jane is missing today. She was also missing at the last meeting. What is this like for you?'

   Some principles here are:

1. Make statements that begin with 'I notice...', owning your observation.

2. Use *direct communication*, keeping statements short and to the point without over-explaining, or the message will get lost in translation.

3. Use metaphor as it enables you to communicate patterns in few words.

4. Use language and a tone of voice that communicates lightness, curiosity and non-judgement.

5. Be open to the team seeing it differently; there is no need to defend your observation or to fight to make it right.

In mode 3, you are using your felt sense, which is a mood, feeling or sensation that is evoked in the coach in the presence of the team. Instead of your attention being directed on the team as in mode 2, you 'submarine' into the depth of your here-and-now experience.

Any team (or individual for that matter) brings their own pattern of relating into the room, and the coach feels the impact of those patterns. The felt sense gives the coach access to a rich set of data which cannot be understood by simply thinking about the situation analytically. It captures the essence of a dynamic moment, which can be gently brought into awareness and understood through collective meaning-making.

> You become aware of a feeling of anxiety. Staying with the feeling, you notice that your shoulders are tight, you are frowning, and your breath is shallow. You stay with the feeling, and what emerges is a sense of inadequacy. You wonder if the work is just too difficult and that you are not a good enough coach. You are aware that you are on the third of six sessions that have been contracted for, so you are over halfway through. You realise this work is going to be a challenge. Given the timeline, the team may not be able to develop as much as they were aiming for. You feel some trepidation and disappointment at the notion that, yet again, a team has unrealistic expectations of what they can achieve in the time they are prepared to invest.

What can you do with this felt sense? There are many ways you can use this data:

➤ You take it to supervision, where you recognise a pattern in yourself of over-promising in order to win the work.

➤ You share it with the team, wondering if your felt sense mirrors the team's in some way. 'I am sensing some anxiety about completing what we set out to do in our work together. Do you know what I mean?' After some nods, you ask, 'I find myself wondering whether this is a common experience for you?' You unpack this together, and the team become aware of a pattern whereby they frequently over-commit and underestimate the time and work involved.

As a coach, you are impacted by the team's ways of being and patterns of relating. You selectively share the thoughts and feelings that arise in you in relation to the team.

Some principles here are:

➤ Pay attention to what is happening *inside yourself* – your own felt sense. It is often more of a background sense than really prominent.

➤ Use 'I am sensing...'

➤ Use language that the team can connect with rather than using coach-speak.

➤ Use mode 3 sparingly, otherwise it loses impact and become too much like the coach's 'touchy-feely style', which is likely to get discounted.

➤ Test the water to see if there is enough psychological safety in the team to process your interventions.

➤ Be curious and non-judgemental in your tone and body language.

➤ Never hold onto 'being right'; if you find yourself stuck in this position, then it is more likely 'your stuff', in which case take it to supervision.

➤ Know yourself. Do the self-work so that you are very familiar and friendly with your own patterns. It will then be easier to acknowledge, in the moment, what might be your own triggers and what might be more of the field.

➤ Your noticing does not always need to be shared in the room; it can be worked with in reflective practice or supervision. If you work as part of a team coaching pair, share your felt sense with each other in support of your own meaning-making and intentional interventions.

There is no right way of using these modes, and how you use them will be infused with your unique presence and coaching style. Experiment with different language, embodiment and tone of voice, and notice the impact you are having. Seek feedback from the team, or your coaching partner, supervisor or peers.

Most of us have our 'go-to' or default mode – the one we use most often, especially when we are feeling insecure or vulnerable. I encourage you to identify your go-to mode and to practise other modes in turn so that you can develop greater range in your practice.

If you pair with another coach, then adopting different modes in the room is helpful as it is impossible to helicopter and submarine at the same time. You can do one or the other, and switch between, but not both.

Finally, the more you use mode 1, the more the team is likely to become reliant on you to facilitate them. When someone leads, others step back to be led. Remember that an effective team learns to lead itself and therefore manages its own process, so when you regularly use mode 1 and facilitate the team, you have probably taken on the role of meeting facilitator, and the team is unlikely to function well without you.

The art of use of self includes selectively sharing observations that seem most pertinent for heightening awareness of the team's characteristic patterns of behaviour. These observations may be about what is happening around you and in the team, and also about what is going on inside you. It is courageous work as it requires us to take personal risks in naming a phenomenon of which the team is potentially unaware, or even avoiding. Naming our own experience can feel vulnerable; however, any change involves risk, and so it is therefore necessary and worthwhile.

To help coaches to understand this skill, at the Studio we developed a simple model (adapted from gestalt psychology) called TDR: Tracking, Describing and Responding.

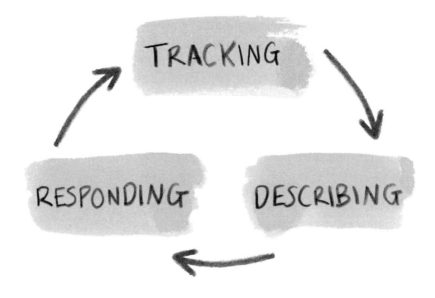

Tracking

In a very practical sense, this means observing a) patterns in the team's interaction, b) how the team is responding to the situation and c) what is going on inside you. For example, you may notice:

➤ the quality of conversation and team dialogue

➤ the levels of engagement and energy

➤ the interactional patterns and team dynamics

➤ the quality of connection and relationships

➤ the levels of awareness

➤ the effectiveness of the team's process (how they are working together)

➤ their capacity for self-regulation as a team.

At the same time, you are tuning into what is evoked in you. You may notice your thoughts, feelings and sensations, like tightness in your body, tingling in your fingers, a knot in your stomach or feeling your energy drop.

Describing

Here, you describe what you have noticed, staying with what is immediately obvious in your awareness. Describe what you have tracked about the team and what you are experiencing yourself (thoughts, feelings or sensations). The challenge here is to describe it without interpreting. This enables the team to stay in the experience, rather than shifting to talking 'about' their experience more conceptually.

Here are some examples of noticing without interpretation:

➤ 'You were frowning as you talked about being excited about this opportunity.'

➤ 'People are often speaking at the same time.'

➤ 'Sue, you said "We could ask our direct reports" three times and nobody responded.

The same statements with interpretation might be:

➤ 'You were frowning as you talked about being excited, so you don't really mean what you are saying.'

➤ 'You are so keen to get your views heard that you don't listen to anyone else.'

➤ 'Sue, no one seems interested in your perspective.'

Describing what you notice without evaluation or interpretation is actually quite challenging and takes some practice. Humans are meaning-making creatures, and the way we make meaning is by interpreting data. So, this is a step that most of us need to practise repeatedly.

Responding

Flowing from tracking and describing, this is about tuning in and disclosing what is being evoked in you. When I say 'evoked', I mean your reactions to the team and the situation. This might be in the form of images or metaphors, or bodily sensations like a tightness in your neck or tingling in your fingers. It may also be emotions that are stirred in you. Some examples:

➤ 'As you have been talking about the future for your business, I have become aware of an image of a flock of birds migrating. Does this have any meaning for you in relation to your future?'

➤ 'When you said that, I got goosebumps up my arms and I imagine that you did too. If so, what might this mean for you?'

➤ 'I notice that you said "We could ask our direct reports" three times and nobody responded. I feel a strong desire to know how your words landed for others.'

TDR is especially powerful in team coaching when you use it to heighten the team's awareness of emerging patterns, either between team members or between you and the team. A 'pattern' is a habitual way of relating. Do they tend to sit quietly and wait to be asked to speak up? Do they wait for the leader to make decisions? Do they talk over one another? Do they listen and build on each other's ideas? Do they challenge everything you say?

You will alienate the team if you share everything you observe, so the art lies in selectively choosing what to disclose in the service of their desired learning and growth. Nevis (1987) wrote: 'What each will be able to attend to will vary, and what each will allow to come into awareness will be different.' Wait patiently, observing with soft eyes until a clear pattern or theme arises. 'Soft eyes' means that, instead of pushing or trying to make something happen, you sit back and relax, slow or stop the chatter in your mind and let events occur, observing without reacting. When waiting with soft eyes, you give your ego a break – your preconceived ideas, stories, judgements and need to perform – in order to discover what is occurring right now. When you use 'hard eyes' you concentrate on one thing; with soft eyes you expand your vision and take in more of the whole, watching the dance instead of the dancer.

Now, let's put all this together:

> You are coaching the top team of a private equity partnership specialising in the retail sector. One of the team of four's primary functions is to assess and make decisions around key investments and acquisitions. Part of your agreed approach is to observe the team on various occasions at their regular partnership meetings. You notice that meetings start up to half an hour late, they are frequently interrupted by calls, and they launch into topics randomly with no agreed agenda or clarity around the desired outcome from each topic discussed. At the third meeting, you observe: Simon says that retail is going nowhere and that they should diversify into a different sector. Tom immediately opposes this view saying they are retail experts and they don't have the expertise to pivot. Jake then gets up and leaves the room to take a call. Simon and Tom continue to assert their own positions. Sharon sits silently, doodling on her notepad. Jake returns after ten minutes and says 'Right, let's talk about fund yield', changing the subject.

> **What are you drawn to?**
> **What intervention will you make?**

This was a real life situation, and I was the coach. I said, 'I have been sitting here with you, and I noticed Simon suggest diversifying; Tom disagreed, saying you should stick to your realm of expertise; Jake left the room for ten minutes; and Sharon said nothing. As I observe this, I find myself feeling quite anxious and wondering what it will

MASTERING THE ART OF TEAM COACHING

take for you all to get on the same page as a team. Does this make any sense to you?'

A few useful guidelines for use of self are:

➤ Tune in to *self*, *team* and the *situation* (STS).

➤ Selectively disclose.

➤ Trust that your disclosure is valid.

➤ Check the impact on the team.

➤ Let go of your reaction or the need to be right.

Consideration for the coach

Many coaches have some personal resistance to use of self in coaching. They are concerned that this might take the focus away from the client, or that their thoughts and feelings are not relevant. They may be concerned about looking stupid, or fearful that they don't know how to 'get it right' or intervene skilfully enough.

We don't see the world in terms of reality; we see it through our own lens. We see things depending on our age, gender, race, history, professional identity and so on. We see things that resonate with our beliefs and judgements, and our hopes and fears. We see things that confirm our own hurts and scars and our own needs and what we yearn for. So, what *you* pay attention to – 'the figure' – is not what *I* pay attention to. Neither of us are wrong; we are both paying attention to different figures. When you realise this, you can let go of the need to be right or to make a perfect intervention. Instead, you offer up your self-experience, with the aim of it being useful and without attachment.

Effecting change

To effect change as a team coach, you model different ways of being, thinking and behaving. However, if you are too different, effectiveness can be compromised as the client focuses on your difference rather than the work at hand. If you are too alike, you can get absorbed into the system. Being seen as similar enough serves to establish relationships, trust and credibility. You do this by expressing appreciation, asking informed questions and affirming the team's perspectives.

Once connection is made, you have more opportunity to differentiate. Now you can begin to challenge assumptions, offer a different perspective and draw attention to the team's patterns of interaction that may be hindering progress. Again, you can take a risk here using a more provocative presence and observe the team's response. This enables you to grade your interventions to the team and the situation.

I often think 'How much provocation can the team tolerate at this time?' and seek to work at that edge. Some teams are so political or so strongly defended that even the smallest provocation can bring up the drawbridge or bring forth the cannons. If this happens, dial down your provocative presence and continue to work on building a relationship with the team through joining and connecting. When you sense that the relationship is strengthened, dial up the provocateur and test the water again. A really useful mantra in a team coach's stance is to 'meet the client where they are at' or to 'start where the system is'.

Building on presence and use of self are active experiments. Together these form a methodology for choice and change.

Active experiments

> All life is an experiment. The more experiments you make, the better.
>
> – RALPH WALDO EMERSON, Journal

Presence and use of self are powerful because they heighten awareness. Without awareness, there is no choice and no change. Adapted from gestalt psychology, our approach to active experiments converts insight into action, where the rubber meets the road. Just talking about change in reality changes little. Instead of teaching the team a concept and hoping they will translate it to their normal working lives, coach them to try it in the here-and-now.

Experiments enable the team to try out new ways of working with no obligation to make the experiment permanent. They provide opportunities for the team to increase their awareness, experience something different and take choiceful action towards their learning goals.

Experiments are emergent and based on a presenting need

If you are present with a team without giving them exercises or prescribing how they work together (mode 1), the team's habituated patterns of working together will naturally emerge. Many coaches primarily use mode 1, in which they are leading the process by instructing the team what to do and how to do it. When you say 'Discuss what you want from today's session. Let's do a round where each person shares in turn', you are directing the traffic and inviting each car to take a turn around the circuit. Alternatively, when you invite the team to discuss what they want from today's session and don't tell them how (share in turn), the team will revert to a more habituated pattern of relating. The system is revealing itself – you just needed to get out of the way!

In teams, many patterns turn into norms, such as:

➤ how they run meetings

➤ how they manage time

➤ how they have dialogue

➤ how they make decisions

➤ how they work through conflict, or don't

➤ how they communicate with each other

➤ how they communicate with various stakeholders.

To be effective as a team, they need effective processes. When there are poor processes or a certain skill is absent, there is a void, and a presenting need is revealed. By practising, refining and embedding effective processes, the team's capacity grows, and they naturally become much more effective and productive. The energy and collective wisdom get channelled into the decisions they need to make and the tasks they need to perform, rather than in struggling to be heard or revisiting decisions over and over again.

Once awareness is raised, you give the team the choice to 'try something different' in the form of an experiment. Experiments can either be designed by the team, co-created by you and the team together or proposed by you. You can introduce tools and exercises to a team, such as talking stick rounds or decision-making frameworks. While these can be useful, they are less experimental as the coach is coming from a place of 'here is what works' rather than 'let's discover what might work'. If you do propose an experiment, be inventive and use your imagination and intuition rather than wheeling out the same old exercises. Ask yourself: what is the unique need that has revealed itself, and what experiment can they try to meet that need?

There is no one right way; however, there will be a way that is effective for the team. Active experiments enable the team to find *what works for them*, rather than what the textbook says they should do, or how you think they should work.

Creating experiments

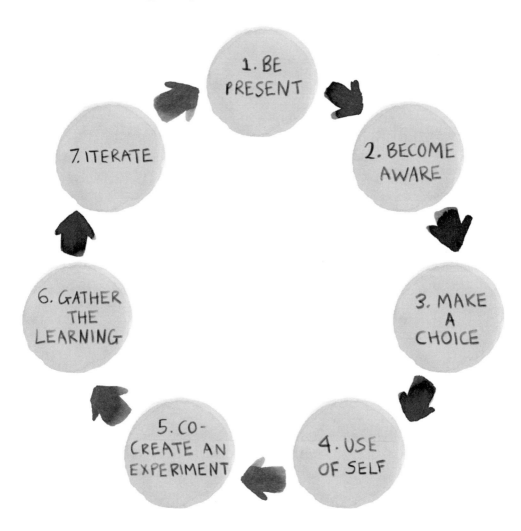

The sequence for active experiments

The best experiments in team coaching are small and simple. Through trial and error, the team gradually embeds valuable processes for collaboration in line with their values and what works for them. Active experiments naturally follow on from the metaskills of presence and use of self. The steps are as follows:

The sequence for active experiments

1. **Be present:** first, get present. Ground and centre yourself. Be in the moment, letting go of your need to make anything happen.

2. **Become aware:** relaxed waiting. With soft eyes, flow your awareness across self, team and the situation.

3. **Make a choice:** pick a pattern or theme that you have noticed.

4. **Use of self:** to name the figure that you notice to heighten the team's awareness. Use modes 2 and/or 3. Check in with the team to see how this landed and whether they have sufficient collective interest to work on this.

5. **Co-create an experiment:** work with the team to design an experiment to 'try something different'.

6. **Gather the learning:** explore what worked and didn't work from the experiment and extract the learning.

7. **Iterate:** if desired, make adjustments and run the experiment again.

Here is an example of the sequence of these metaskills in action:

A team of eight senior managers in a technology business agreed that one of their learning goals was to improve how they communicate as a team. They became completely focused on operational issues and were tolerating poor quality group processes and interactions.

I shared my observations: 'I notice you often interrupt each other and rarely acknowledge or build on each other's contributions. Also, you have opened up several topics at a time without closing any off. I am finding this a little frustrating; it could just be me, but I wonder how it is for you? If you were to rate the quality of communication between you on a scale from 1 to 5, what would it be?'

One by one, they shared their scores; the highest was a 3, so their awareness was raised. I asked what difference improving this score would make to both their performance and their enjoyment of working together as a team. They agreed it would be really valuable. Now, they were aligned around a collective theme and willing to work on it. I asked them what experiment they could create to improve their score. They agreed to listen to each other and check for understanding before adding in their own views. They also decided to pick up one of the open topics and to see it through to conclusion. After running this experiment for ten minutes, we paused to check how it was going. All reported a 5, with the exception of one team member who said 4, qualifying that ten minutes wasn't enough. They agreed to repeat with the next topic for 15 minutes.

I hope that now you will see that active experiments can be remarkably small and simple.

Testing the water

One of the things to consider is that what is available to one team is not to another, meaning that the same experiments won't work with every team. We have already discussed that teams need good enough psychological safety to be prepared to experiment and take risks and, if there is not enough safety or the risk seems too high, they will resist trying anything. Sometimes our experiments as coaches are perceived as too weird for the team and their culture. If your experiment is too 'out there' and different from the team's accepted norms and culture (e.g. 'How about you all sing this song and see if you can harmonise with one another?'), then the team is likely to bring up the drawbridge. On the other hand, if you don't bring enough difference, you will have limited impact. So grade your experiments, testing the water to see what the team will respond to. Seek to work at the edge of their comfort zone, asking yourself how much provocation the team can tolerate at this moment in time.

Principles for using active experiments

When using active experiments, consider the following principles:

➤ Create experiments around a presenting need that emerges in the moment.

➤ Designing an experiment is a co-creative process.

➤ Take an experimental attitude; all outcomes are valuable.

➤ Try something new and untested to determine what is possible.

➤ Experiments involve risk-taking: the outcomes are unknown.

➤ Test the water and grade experiments towards the edge of the team's comfort zone.

➤ Don't aim for the 'magic wand experiment' – one designed to provide a perfect solution. If you find yourself doing this, you are not fully present, and you are probably working too hard.

➤ Let the team do the work!

Reflection time

Metaskills sit at the centre of our approach to team coaching. A key element of this 'inside-out' model is our presence as a team coach. We all have presence, whether we recognise it or not. How we show up is unique, so it makes sense to know more about it so we can make maximum use of it. Try the exercise earlier in this chapter to discover more about your presence.

You can also:

➤ Recall moments when you have acted out of character.

➤ Recall moments outside of your work when you can be quite different to your work self.

What is different? How would you describe your presence in these moments? (You may uncover many dimensions.)

Give yourself permission to experiment with and incorporate these dimensions into your work. Notice the impact the shift has on your clients and the situation.

Carry out the following reflective exercise to understand your presence more fully when you are coaching teams:

➤ Describe your presence as if talking to a seven-year-old child. Keep your language simple.

➤ Ask co- or paired team coaches you have worked with to describe your presence during team coaching. What words and language do they use to describe it?

Repeat this exercise, this time seeking feedback and input from client teams to describe your presence. Then ask yourself:

➤ Do you have the presence you might need for a given team coaching assignment?

➤ What aspects of your presence might you benefit from dialling up or down during team coaching?

Remember: presence is developable, and we can all learn to extend the range of our presence as team coaches. Track your presence and notice how it changes over time. It is one of your best team coaching tools and completely unique. Make it work harder for you.

Use of self is similarly personal to each of us as team coaches. Ask yourself:

➤ To what degree is the use of self metaskill part of your team coaching repertoire?

➤ How might your team coaching benefit from incorporating it?

➤ What is your use of self as a team coach? Do you use emotions as data and where do you experience this? Physically in your embodied self or more cognitively through observations?

Make a note of your last three team coaching assignments. Ask yourself:

➤ Which modes (1,2,3) did you use? What informed your choice of mode (habit or intentional choice)?

➤ Which modes did you not use?

➤ Which modes do you actively avoid? What can you learn from this?

➤ What difference would active experiments make to your team coaching practice?

Try making use of experiments in your team coaching work and notice what happens. Choose a team to try this with, contract for it and give it a go, responding to a team's needs 'in the moment.' What did you learn from this and how will you adapt your approach to team coaching as a result?

6 Team Coaching Competencies

Where one-to-one coaching is about the quality of the conversation between coach and client, team coaching is about the quality of conversation between team members.

– ALLARD DE JONG

Professional coaches worldwide will be familiar with the concept of coaching competencies. They underpin most coach training programmes and provide a framework for the assessment of coaches undergoing professional accreditation. During my own development as a coach, the International Coaching Federation (ICF) Core Competencies served as a compass, offering me guidance and direction towards coaching mastery. I reviewed session recordings against this competency framework, observing my strengths and the skills that I needed to practise. I worked with skilful mentor coaches who enabled me to notice my blind spots and to sharpen my learning edge. Competencies brought coaching to life for me and challenged me to really get the skills in my bones.

Generally, coaches first encounter coaching competencies during their foundational coach training. As they progress, deepening their understanding of these enables coaches to embed them in their coaching until they flow naturally. However, the competencies frameworks we all embrace were designed with one-to-one coaching in mind. When working with teams, coaches need all of the individual coaching competencies, but they also need more to guide this complex and messy work.

Teams exist within organisational systems which are continually changing. In individual coaching, success is defined by the coachee (sometimes with sponsor input) and the mindset and behaviours that shape performance reside within them. That person defines their own goals and determines the actions they will take to achieve these goals. Learning is also integrated at the individual level and, even when the individual coaching is funded by the organisation, very little of the learning derived from the coaching is propagated across the organisation.

In team coaching, however, success may be defined by the team, team leader, the organisation or their stakeholders – or a combination thereof. For a team to be effective, it needs to harness the energy of a group of people towards a common purpose or set of goals. Team members discuss and debate different ideas and opinions and, ultimately, align on decisions. They hold each other to account for their actions, and success often relies on many moving parts that are rarely under one person's control. Also, their operating assumptions and team processes (how they work together) are often inhibitors of their collective performance.

For me, the lack of a competency framework for team coaching presented both an ethical and professional dilemma. I am committed to professional standards and have personally invested hundreds of hours in training and thousands of hours of practice to get accredited as an ICF Master Certified Coach. I craved a clear enough compass to guide my work. So, along with colleagues at the TCS, I developed the TCS Team Coaching Wheel (see Chapter 5) as a guide for ourselves and other professional coaches. I believe that we were the first organisation globally to develop a set of professional team coaching competencies, and they have stood us in good stead as trainers and practitioners over the years.

Thankfully, the two largest professional bodies, the ICF and the AC, are well on their way to providing accreditation for team coaches. I say this with delight and gratitude as Declan Woods and myself, along with other colleagues, have been campaigning for several years for professional guidance that team coaches urgently need. I am sure that the TCS Team Coaching Wheel has contributed greatly to the frameworks that we will eventually see used in practice.

TCS Team Coaching Wheel

At the heart of the wheel lies the philosophy and stance of a team coach, which we explored in Chapter 3. These provide a bedrock of principles, assumptions and mantras that support us in *being* a team coach.

The next layer contains the transformational metaskills of presence, use of self and active experiments, which together provide us with a methodology for change. Many one-to-one coaches learned the GROW model (standing for Goal, Reality, Options, Will), which provides structure and flow to coaching conversations. In team coaching, the metaskills provide this flow as they are focused on the collaborative nature of teamwork.

The third layer contains the team coaching competencies, which are organised into five clusters: a) Setting the Foundation, b) Co-creating the Relationship, c) Fostering Effective Communication, d) Working with Systems & Dynamics and e) Facilitating Learning & Growth. In the coming chapters, we will explore each cluster in turn.

Reflection time

Competencies form the bedrock of professional team coaching. They can help educate organisational sponsors about what team coaching is, explain what constitutes good professional practice and inform buying decisions about team coaching services. They can also inform the design and delivery of providers' team coach training programmes.

For team coaches, competencies can illustrate core elements of team coaching practice and bring new(er) aspects into awareness and, by using behavioural language, help put these into practice.

Coaches can use competency models to plan their ongoing coach development. In chapters 7-11, we look at the competencies in more detail. After reading these, you might want to carry out a basic audit of your current team coaching practice. Rate yourself on a scale of 0 to 10 (with ten being the highest) of your current level of effectiveness against the following five clusters:

1. Setting the Foundation

2. Co-creating the Relationship

3. Fostering Effective Communication

4. Working with Systems & Dynamics

5. Facilitating Learning & Growth.

Then ask yourself:

➤ Which competencies are you using/not using?

➤ Which competencies are you using the most? Why is this?

➤ Which competencies are you using the least? Why is this?

➤ Which competencies would benefit from the most development in improving your coaching work with teams?

Develop your competence as a team coach by:

➤ journaling and making reflective notes on your practice and development

➤ keeping a simple log of your ongoing team coaching development.

All of the professional coaching bodies are developing team coach accreditation or credentialling schemes, and will most likely ask you to keep a record of your training and development as a team coach as part of your accreditation portfolio. It will be easier if you record these activities as you go along. Plan for your ongoing team coaching development by asking yourself:

➤ What do I need to learn? (You could use the team coaching competencies as a guide.)

➤ What activity will I undertake to help with this learning? (e.g. targeted reading; skill development (against the competencies); supervision; participating in a masterclass or further training, etc.)

➤ What have I learned from completing this team coach development activity?

➤ How will I integrate this learning into my team coaching methodology and practice?

7 Setting the Foundation

You're only as solid as what you build on.

The coaching journey begins with Setting the Foundation – laying the ground on which all coaching relationships are built. Any practising coach will have discovered to their cost the unintended impact of laying poor foundations as the subsequent work relies on this. Without adequate underpinning, the work will inevitably wobble or collapse.

In the Setting the Foundation cluster, there are two core competencies that weave together to provide a good grounding for team coaching: *ethical practice* and *contracting*.

Competency 1: Ethical Practice

It doesn't matter how well trained you are or how many stripes you have on your shirt; if you're not ethical you can potentially do harm to your coachee.

– ALLARD DE JONG (2006)

At TCS, we simply define *ethical practice* as: 'Understanding coaching ethics and standards and applying them in all team coaching situations.' It is demonstrated by these three behaviours:

➤ **Understanding and exhibiting team coaching ethics and behaviours (as defined by your professional body).**

➤ **Clearly communicating the distinctions between coaching, consulting, facilitating, training, group therapy and other professions that provide support and development to teams.**

➤ **Referring the client to another team coach, or support professional, as and when needed, and resources are available.**

De Jong says, 'sound ethics are the essence and underpinning of good coaching', and 'people acting as professional coaches must adhere to the highest standards of responsibility and accountability to protect the interests of the coachee'. An ethical code provides appropriate guidelines and enforceable standards of conduct for coach, client and the profession.

The leading professional bodies have established codes of ethics for coaches. These codes describe the core values, ethical principles and ethical standards of behaviour for professional coaches. I recommend that you read and digest the code of ethics of your chosen professional body on a regular basis as they serve to uphold the integrity of the coaching profession by a) clarifying standards of conduct consistent with the core values and ethical principles of coaching, and b) guiding ethical reflection, education and decision-making.

There is considerable consistency between the codes, and while not exhaustive, I have drawn out ten standards here for our consideration as team coaches:

1. Ensure your client understands the nature and potential value of team coaching.

2. Agree roles, responsibilities and rights of all parties involved.

3. Maintain appropriate and clear boundaries of confidentiality.

4. Transparently manage any conflicts of interest.

5. Address any indication that there might be a shift in value received from the team coaching relationship.

6. Be aware of and address any power or status difference between coach and client that might be caused by cultural, relational, psychological or contextual issues.

7. Commit to excellence through continued personal, professional and ethical development.

8. Represent your coaching qualifications and your level of competence truthfully and accurately.

9. Engage in supervision with a suitably qualified team coaching supervisor with a frequency appropriate to your coaching.

10. Systematically evaluate the quality of your work through client, peer, mentor and supervisor feedback.

The real challenge for all coaches is to consistently walk the path of *ethical practice* in every coaching relationship and interaction. The very nature of an ethical dilemma is that it implies a situation where there is no easy choice or answer; and it can be agonising trying to decide what is best and to act on this decision by taking ethical action.

Here's a real experience that I had.

More time passed, and the circle of debate was getting smaller and more heated. I felt tension building as several team members pulled back, silently observing. The conversation was now centred between Soren, the CEO, Glyn the marketing director and Jim, a long-standing divisional director. Curt, the finance director, chipped in with the occasional comment critiquing the ideas proposed. Each time he spoke out, I noticed Soren give a short puff of breath and turn his head away. This continued for another 15 minutes or so, and the energy was dissipating. Soren had lost his usual calm gravitas, and instead his voice was clipped with frustration. In the end, after one more interjection from Curt, Soren snapped at him.

'Cut the cynicism, Curt. You need to decide whether you're on this bus or off it. In fact, you need to realise it's not a f**king bus, it's a Ferrari.'

Soren and Curt stared at each other. The room went silent. Several pairs of eyes turned to Anita, the people director, who was sitting quietly observing. They seemed to be saying, 'Don't just sit there, do something', calling her to act.

'I think we all need to calm down a bit,' she finally said, flushing slightly and looking fixedly at the water bottle in front of her.

I watched in horror as Soren picked up a book from the table in front of him and hurled it at her, yelling, 'That goes for you too Anita, get a backbone!'

Soren walked determinedly out of the room, saying he was taking a break and he would be back in five. A pall of embarrassment fell. Anita also left the room, one hand touching the side of her head where the book had struck her. Curt stood up and went to the coffee station.

The challenge of committing to *ethical practice* means that you will inevitably encounter situations that require you to respond. It can take real courage to make the 'right' decision and to act on it. How would you respond to this situation? What values, principles or standards inform your choice?

My mind was racing as fast as my heart. I knew that this was a critical moment and, if I was to offer anything useful to this team, I needed to show some grit. I was also deeply aware of the fragility of the situation as I had not gained the team's trust or even contracted with them yet around how we were going to work together. I focused on grounding myself and quietening the clamour in my mind.

Soren returned to the room; Anita did not. A glimmer of shock crossed his face as he remembered I was in the room. Turning to me he said, 'Don't make too much of that, we have a tough culture here and we all need to man up.' Looking him in the eye, I stood up saying 'I would like to take a moment' and, turning to the team, I said, 'What just happened?' following with 'Turn to the person next to you and discuss for five minutes. After a few moments of uncertainty, they did as I asked. Privately to Soren I said, 'This could be the most valuable conversation with the team you have ever had, so I am asking you to trust me.'

When the time was up, I asked the team to share the most significant things from their discussions with the team as a whole, and I was encouraged by their comments.

Jim went first: 'Soren is under a lot of pressure from the board and we need to work with him, not against him.' Glyn followed: 'I agree, and we need to generate some breakthrough ideas, just doing the same will get us the same results.'

Gradually more people spoke up, one saying, 'But we need to listen to Curt as he sees what we don't see' and another, 'We need to listen to each other, as we are going around in circles and not getting anywhere.'

After a few more comments, I thanked them for responding to my question and then said, 'I notice that no one has mentioned Anita and the fact that she had a book thrown at her.' At this point, most people looked at the floor and a few eyes were on Soren. I was aware of psychological safety and concerned that the container may not yet be strong enough to hold the tension. I needed to meet the team where they were and to use my presence. Looking around the room at each person one by one, I said 'I know it can be hard to talk about this together as a team, but if you rise to the occasion you will begin to become the team that you aspire to be. Have courage.'

There was another silence until one of the long-standing divisional directors spoke up, 'Soren is frustrated with Anita as he thinks she needs to step up her game. He let it get the better of him and threw the book. He does lose his temper like we all do, but it's the first time he's done anything like that.' He looked at Soren.

'You are right. I shouldn't have done that. I am just really feeling the pressure. We have come so far and been really successful but, in all honesty, I don't know if we can continue with this level of growth year on year. The more successful we are, the more the board expects.' Turning to leave the room he said, 'I'll go and find Anita and apologise.'

This baptism of fire taught me many lessons. The most valuable is that, in team coaching, I am the tool. It is less about the right question but the presence and skill with which you use it. In this situation, matching Soren's hierarchical power with my own presence enabled me to host the space and to work with what came up. You can learn to do the same.

If you discuss dilemmas with team coaching peers, you will quickly discover there is no one right answer. A professional code of ethics offers us guidance but cannot possibly direct us on each and every situation. While many coaches share the core values described above, we also each have our own 'principled conscience' – our personal hierarchy of values. The importance of supervision in ethical reflection and decision-making is paramount as it provides us with another perspective to our own, one which is guided by experience and professional practice. Supervision can illuminate our blind spots, challenge our integrity and support us in finding the courage to have the difficult conversations that ethical dilemmas inevitably call upon team coaches to have.

 Visit the book website for further examples of ethical dilemmas and how different coaches responded.

Competency 2: Contracting

You cannot NOT make contracts!

Every coaching engagement includes a coaching agreement – a contract – between coach and client. The agreement may involve other stakeholders, such as the client's line manager, HR partner or both. It may be formal or informal, explicit or implicit. In team coaching, contracting is more complex as often multiple interconnected relationships exist, each with different hopes and expectations from the coaching. The team coaching contract is an essential element of the coaching relationship requiring considered thought and action.

So, what exactly is a team coaching contract? It is an agreement made between the coach and the team (and often, the organisation) concerning their work together and their working relationship, otherwise called a *working alliance*. It can be tempting to reduce contracting to a simple model or checklist to work through at the beginning of a new assignment, but the reality is that contracting happens throughout the coaching relationship. There are many forms of contracting in team coaching, from the initial contract for 'the work' to the subtle navigation of the ongoing and evolving team coaching relationship.

Any human relationship is founded on explicit and implicit agreements about how we exist in relationship to one another. Think about any relationship in your life, be it with a partner, friend, parent, sibling, colleague, client, boss, teacher and so on; each relationship has its own contracts. However, most of these are formed implicitly, through the lived experience of the relationship. You cannot *not* make contracts! In team coaching, a lack of explicit contracting is highly likely to lead to problems.

The six Ps of contracting

There are different types of contracting in team coaching. At TCS, we identified six areas of contracting in team coaching organised into the Six Ps of Contracting in Team Coaching model below:

The Six Ps of Contracting in Team Coaching

Purpose

The purpose for team coaching is the driving reason behind it. Clarifying the purpose for any coaching relationship is essential. We might ask questions like:

➤ Why are we coming together?

➤ What change is desired and by whom?

➤ What is the picture of success?

➤ How will success be measured?

The questions are simple enough, so surely this part of contracting must be straightforward?

Clarifying the purpose for team coaching is like looking through a kaleidoscope at a multicoloured and constantly changing image. If you ask one person, say the team leader, you may be presented with a clear enough picture. However, the purpose may be defined by a combination of stakeholders, such as the team's sponsor (HR or L&D), the team leader, individual team members, the team leader's boss, the organisation's top team (board, executive team, partners, etc.), direct reports and customers. The purpose is highly likely to differ for each stakeholder depending on the lens they are looking through! As with a kaleidoscope, a team coach may need to bring together a whole spectrum of perspectives to create a shared picture of success for the work.

Having arrived at a clear purpose, you may feel some relief. As humans, we are wired towards clarity and a reasonable degree of certainty. Beware, as you may well find that the purpose of the coaching changes as the team gains greater awareness of their situation and potential. After all, some people have never experienced a great team and are therefore unaware of what can be achieved.

Another reason the purpose of the team coaching may change is that, in this fast-paced and volatile world, everything around is us constantly changing. New pressures and opportunities emerge over the course of a team coaching programme, and this can change the focus of the work. So, be sure to regularly check in on the purpose for team coaching as it may well alter over the course of a programme.

I was coaching a newly formed top team in local government where team members were senior leaders from two separate and now merged organisations. The team and their major stakeholders, the political leader and cabinet, were in full agreement about the purpose of the team coaching: 'to support the senior leadership team in coming together to lead the organisation as one cohesive team'.

A few months later, the pandemic hit. The purpose of the team coaching shifted: 'to support the SLT in becoming agile and resilient in leading the organisation through the crisis'. They recognised that this crisis was temporary and that they also needed to lead the organisation to deliver better outcomes for the public in their region, so they agreed to revisit the purpose of the team coaching as the context shifted.

Beware of our need for certainty as it can mask the reality that new data emerges, requiring the team coaching contract to change.

Practical

Sometimes referred to as the 'administrative' or 'business' contract, this type of contract deals with all practicalities such as the venue, time, frequency of sessions, the duration of the team coaching programme, fees and payment terms, logistics, cancellations, missed sessions or termination of the team coaching.

The *practical* contract also deals with explicit boundaries of confidentiality. This is important in any coaching relationship, but it is equally important and also more complex in team coaching. The specific confidentiality agreements you make will be down to your *ethical practice* and your methodology. Your level of skill at managing boundaries is also a key consideration. Some factors when considering the boundaries of confidentiality are:

➤ Will you be providing coaching to individual team members or the team leader, as well as the team? Will information from any one-to-one conversations be shared with the whole team? If so, by whom?

➤ Will you be gathering data from stakeholders, either by interview or electronic surveys or some other means? With whom will the data be shared? Will it be anonymous or named?

➤ Is there a sponsor such as HR or L&D who is not a team member but who expects to be privy to any data?

Finally, what are the boundaries around confidentiality if you, as team coach, become aware of harmful behaviour like bullying? Imagine what it would be like to have agreed total confidentiality with a team, only to discover that the leader is a terrible bully. What about suspicious, fraudulent or illegal activity?

Professional

The professional contract defines what you are offering as a team coach, and what you are not. What does the team want and need from you as their coach? How competent are you at meeting those needs? What qualifications and experience do you bring? What are the limits of your skills and competence?

For example, you are told that the team – a board of directors – wants to start the team coaching with a comprehensive psychometric assessment of the team. You may well be certified in various assessment tools, but are they expecting you to evaluate team members and to advise on their fitness for roles? This may put you into an advisory role, rather than one of team coach.

It can be very helpful to offer a definition of team coaching and what can be expected of your role, and what is expected of the team and team leadership.

Finally, the *professional* contract also covers any professional code of ethics that you subscribe to. We recommend that team coaches provide clients with a copy of this code as part of the onboarding process.

Power

Every organisational system has a power system. Often implicit or unnamed, it configures the field within which the team coaching will take place and shapes the whole team coaching process.

A 'power system' is about authority and how decisions are made. In some organisations and teams, the inherent culture is top down, and the leader holds tightly to their authority rather than sharing it with team members. The leadership style is often 'hub and spoke' whereby all decisions are made by one individual – the hub. The spokes are team members who are managed individually by the leader, and information flows through the leader. So, if one team member has an issue with another, often the complaint will be communicated to the leader to 'deal with'.

Other organisations or teams operate more on the basis of distributed power where decisions are made collectively, and team members assume leadership responsibility across the whole of the team. This means that team members offer and provide support and challenge to one another, rather than via a single leader.

Of course, there are teams that espouse shared leadership, but the power is actually held by one or perhaps two individuals. And there are teams that are a hybrid where the leader assumes decision-making authority for the 'what' – the vision and purpose of the team – and team members collectively decide on the 'how'.

Many team coaches have egalitarian values and aspire to every organisation operating through consensus or collective leadership, wanting equal voice and fairness for everyone. This can become disruptive in team coaching, as coaches can find themselves at odds with the power system of the team and their organisation. Remember, team coaches work to the client's agenda, and your client – the team – has its own power system. Understanding this system will tell you who you need to be contracting with and why, who sets the agenda and who will make decisions along the way about timing, spend, the focus of the coaching, and so on.

Psychological

Less commonly discussed is the psychological contract, meaning what is secret, hidden or undiscovered. There are three categories of internal dialogue that are usually in the minds of team members at the start of team coaching:

About themselves: Why am I here? How do I want to be? What's expected of me? How can I protect myself?

About the coach: Why are you here? How do I want you to be? Do I trust you? How 'scary' are you? How much do I need to protect myself?

About the outcomes: Is this going to be a worthwhile use of time? Do I need to fit this in alongside everything else? What are we hoping to achieve?

As team members' internal dialogue is often unspoken, your aim as team coach is to find a graceful way to surface and address underlying needs and concerns in a way that creates safety and builds the container.

Begin by noticing. How do people enter the room? What are they wearing? What are they talking about? What does the 'energy' feel like in the room? What might this 'tell' around the nature of the contracting conversation you need to have?

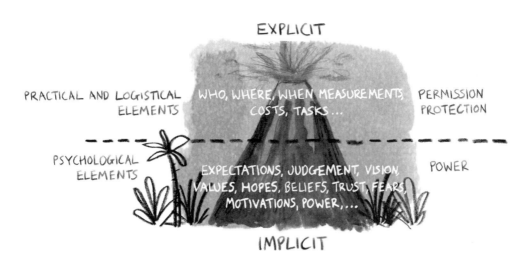

The contracting volcano

As you can see in the 'contracting volcano', tensions occur under the surface, creating pressure inside the system. This pressure can build up to such a degree that unless it is released, 'explosions' happen in the form of toxic behaviours, destructive conflict, in-fighting, power games and more. Skilful team coaches release tension in the system by inviting dialogue with the aim of understanding what lies under the surface; this frees up the team's energy to focus on collaborative work.

The kind of questions that can be helpful to explore are:

➤ **What are the deepest hopes for the team coaching?**

➤ **What expectations need to be expressed (of the leader, individual team members, coach, stakeholders, other)?**

➤ **What would make this a great learning experience?**

➤ **What would make it the opposite?**

➤ **What are people's concerns?**

When working with the psychological contract, the art of team coaching is about a subtle balance of courage and sensitivity. As a coach, you build a safe container by establishing and maintaining clear boundaries, such as keeping to agreements on timings and by communicating directly and respectfully. You then gently test the team's willingness to name what until now has been unsaid, often by asking a less contentious question first like 'What other expectations might you have that have not yet been spoken?' and then moving gradually into deeper water, noticing any resistance and meeting it with curiosity and compassion. I aim never to push through resistance as it is a necessary form of human protection, and our role is not to rip that away but more to create the conditions where the resistance can be understood and worked with. Resistance is usually down to unmet needs, which will need to be sufficiently satisfied for change to happen.

As discussed, confidentiality agreements are part of the professional contract; however, confidentiality is also held implicitly at the psychological level. You may be asking team members to share their thoughts and feelings and what they see as effective and problematic behaviour. They may feel embarrassed about a lack of effectiveness of performance, and they may harbour anger, blame or resentment at other team members, the team leader or others in the organisational system. Creating a safe space is vital in fostering the conditions in which people can be vulnerable.

Developing the psychological contract is not a linear or predictable process. When you work at the edge of the team's comfort zone, there is always risk involved. It is less about a checklist written on a flipchart and more about how you meet the moments that naturally emerge.

Partnership

Team coaches work in partnership with the team they are coaching. As this partnership is based on mutuality, both team members and the coach are equally responsible for creating and developing this relationship. A team coaching contract is an explicit *multilateral commitment* to a *team coaching relationship* and to a *well-defined course of action*. Let's look at what we mean by these:

Multilateral commitment

Multilateral means 'agreed upon by or participated in by three or more parties'. In team coaching there are always at least three parties:

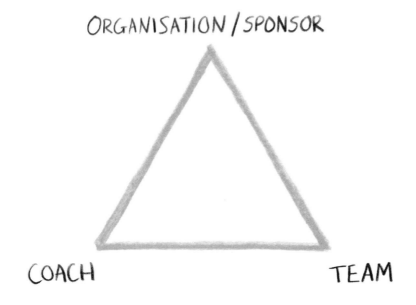

However, the contract may be more complex, for example:

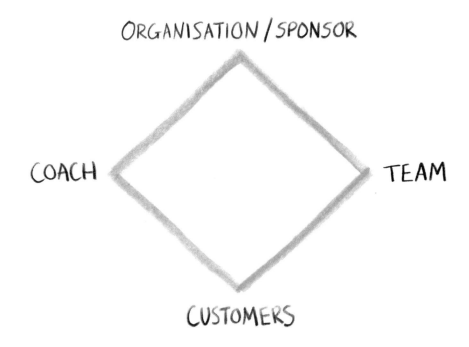

ORGANISATION / SPONSOR

COACH

TEAM

CUSTOMERS

You could continue to build this diagram, adding in other stakeholders such as investors, customers, suppliers, the wider contract, and so on. Depending on the diagram, there are agreements between all those involved, but often these are implied rather than openly stated. Consequently, there may be different perceptions of these agreements, which lead to misunderstandings.

Team coaching relationship

Research demonstrates (De Haan, 2008) that successful outcomes do not depend on the specific theory or methodology of the practitioner, but on the strength of this partnership. In my view, what contributes to the effectiveness of the team coaching relationship is one where:

➤ team members and the team feel understood and attended to

➤ there is mutual trust and respect

➤ there is a shared understanding of 'the work' (the desired outcomes and the team coaching process)

➤ there is 'good enough' commitment across the team to the team and the work.

For more on the team coaching relationship, see Chapter 8: Co-creating the Relationship.

Well-defined course of action

During the initial exploratory discussion, naturally you will explore why the team wants coaching, what has led to the need, and the outcomes that they hope to achieve. This information will all be part of your initial contracting with the team, along with the agreed team coaching programme and process. This is a well-defined course of action.

As you get into the work and meet team members, and perhaps their stakeholders, and start to understand the context better, more data becomes available. This continues through the discovery phase of the team coaching journey, as well as through team coaching and live action coaching sessions. As such, the team's development needs and possible outcomes from the coaching will be emerging throughout and the contract can be updated accordingly.

Team coaches can get into troubled waters when they forget 'ABC' – *Always Be Contracting.* For example, you ask the team, 'What do you want to focus on in this session?', and each team member proposes something different. Do you defer to the team leader to decide, do you invite the team to vote or do you decide? If the team coach simply proposes they put the ideas up on a flipchart and vote on them, then *the coach is choosing* how the decision will be made and is therefore not following the team's agenda. So, in this example, contract with the team: 'I notice you have different views on the area of focus for today's session; how do you want to go about agreeing a way forward?'

Visit the book website for a handout on an example contract for roles (team leader, team member and coach) and other resources on contracting.

Reflection time

Solid foundations are as important in team coaching as they are when building a house.

Ethics can be considered an abstract concept, until you consider the multitude of dilemmas team coaches face. Having a practical way of thinking about and tackling them can prove invaluable for a team coach.

Think about recent team coaching assignments. Identify dilemmas – real or potential – you encountered. List them. Then ask yourself:

➤ What do you notice about these dilemmas? Are there any commonalities? What stands out for you?

➤ How did you tackle them?

➤ What was your approach to addressing them? Would a framework as a way to think about them be useful?

Now map a team you are currently coaching or about to coach, to represent the parties involved in a multilateral contract. You could use dotted lines between parties where the contract is implied rather than stated.

➤ What are the different needs of these parties and how might you respond to them while contracting for team coaching?

➤ What needs to be agreed between these different parties to create a working alliance and how will you reconcile any differences?

➤ If you are currently coaching a team, can you trace any ethical dilemmas back to contracting with a client team? (If you can, you are not alone. This is one of the commonest occurrences in team coaching work.)

➤ What have you learned about ethical practice and contracting, and how will you integrate this learning into your team coaching approach?

8 Co-creating the Relationship

Change happens in the crucible of relationship.

– BILL CRITCHLEY (2010)

Relationships are at the very heart of coaching and, without question, they form the fabric of our lives. We exist in a web of relationships, each with their own histories and needs, influencing our sense of identity and wellbeing.

Take a moment to think about someone who has negatively impacted you. How would you describe your relationship? What do you feel as you recall that person? Now, do the same for someone who has profoundly and positively affected you. Notice the different feelings and sensations that are evoked in you.

These feelings are ingrained in the relationship between you. They affect how we see ourselves, what we believe we are capable of and our sense of what is possible in life. Some relationships evoke the best in you and the most optimistic outlook. In others, you can feel small, unseen or unmet, misjudged and so much less than whole. We learn about who we are and our place in the world in relationship.

In coaching, successful outcomes depend less on the specific theory, techniques, models or tools of the practitioner, and much more on the strength of the coaching relationship (de Haan, 2008; Asay & Lambert, 1999). The coaching relationship is co-created and it serves as a crucible for change. Like alchemists heating base metals to high temperatures inside a crucible, in the hope of creating the elixir of life, the coaching relationship provides a safe container where trans-formation can take place. In team coaching, the relationship crucible needs to be even more substantial to potentially bear extreme heat and chemical reactions.

There are two significant competencies that contribute to co-creating the team coaching relationship: *psychological safety and trust*, and *effective relating*.

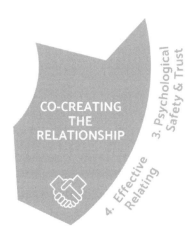

Competency 3: Psychological Safety and Trust

Psychological safety is a function of the group whereas trust is between two individuals. Psychological safety describes an immediate experience while trust is about some future moment.

– STEWART (2019)

The fundamental aim of team coaching is for the team to learn and grow in its capacity to achieve its desired outcomes. Teams

learn through generative dialogue, creating new meaning from divergent thinking, and from new experiences and practice. However, all learning is a vulnerable experience as it takes us out of our familiar comfort zone. When we do not feel safe, our energy is directed towards protecting ourselves and others, often through defensive behaviours. Psychological safety is therefore critical for team learning and change. Without it, team coaching might cause the team to pull up the drawbridge while they make their retreat. However, in a climate of psychological safety, teams can perform and innovate.

What is psychological safety?

All of us will have felt unsafe in a group or team at some point in our lives. As humans, we are social beings, and most people are members of several groups, both formal and informal. So rather than looking for a textbook definition of psychological safety, I invite you to take a moment to reflect on your own experience of being a member of various groups and teams, both in your organisational and personal life.

Recall an experience of not feeling psychologically safe in the group. Perhaps you felt this way every time you were involved with the group, or maybe it was a moment in time over the life cycle of the group. What influenced your experience? Now, take out your journal and write down the factors that made you feel unsafe. Then do the opposite and think of a group where you felt, or feel, very safe. Write down what factors contribute(d) to your sense of safety.

Facing a new global market for students, a prestigious UK university crafted a strategic plan outlining five key goals that would drive performance. This plan was ambitious, and it would require elite performance from the executive team. Success would not be achieved by simply having good people; it would take a conscious and determined effort as a team. To this aim, the HR director proposed some team coaching.

I met with the vice chancellor (VC) and agreed an approach that began with a discovery phase, including an executive team assessment and individual interviews with each team member. The results of the assessment would be initially reviewed with the VC, and then with the team as a whole, with the aim of clarifying the team's development areas.

The data revealed a lack of trust and openness in the team forum. Team members were extremely cautious about speaking out in team meetings, believing it would be career-limiting. They said 'what the headmaster wants to hear' rather than speaking their minds, and it wasn't worth the effort of speaking up anyway, as the VC had already decided what he wanted in advance of any meeting. In reality, conversations were more constructive outside team meetings than in.

As agreed, I met with the vice chancellor to share the themes from the diagnostics. I asked him whether I could speak plainly and he said he was all ears. I said, 'There are many strong themes in the data, not least around the excellent work carried out on the new strategic plan. However, your team are afraid to speak their minds. They feel like they need to anticipate what you want to hear and that you do not value their input into decision-making.' I paused. There was a long silence during which the VC was looking down at the floor with his forehead pressed against steepled fingers. Eventually, he looked up and stared me straight in the eye, and said, 'I pay them to do, not to think', his tone like a slap to my face. I felt myself flushing. I asked, 'But aren't academic institutions all about fostering and valuing independent thinking?' He retorted that he needed them to get on and do their jobs and that if team coaching was about getting them to discuss and debate, he was having none of it.

Harvard researcher Amy Edmondson (1999) defines team psychological safety as 'a shared belief held by members of a team that the team is safe for interpersonal risk taking'. This is not the same as team cohesiveness, which can result in groupthink as, to preserve harmony, team members become unwilling to disagree or challenge others' views. In teams with high psychological safety, members feel confident to speak out without fear of being seen as ignorant, incompetent, negative or disruptive.

See the book website for details of Project Aristotle's research into 'What makes a team effective at Google', building on Edmondson's work. It offers definitions of 'team' and 'effectiveness' as well as some great tools for fostering psychological safety.

To provide more specific guidance for team coaches, at TCS, we define the competency of psychological safety and trust as 'the ability to create a safe and supportive atmosphere for team learning and growth'. The behaviours that support this are:

1. **Creates an environment that encourages ongoing mutual respect and trust of the coaching process.**

2. **Establishes clear agreements, keeps promises and seeks permission to coach in sensitive areas.**

3. **Demonstrates personal integrity, honesty and sincerity and respect for the team's values, beliefs and learning styles.**

4. **Actively engages in open two-way feedback.**

5. **Provides ongoing support for new behaviours supporting risk-taking and fear of failure.**

Team psychological safety goes beyond trust, which has long been recognised as important in group dynamics; it describes a climate of mutual respect and trust in which people are comfortable being themselves.

Creating a container

> You cannot work 'on' a field. But you can create a 'container'.
>
> – WILLIAM ISAACS (1999)

A container is a 'vessel' in which the dynamics and undercurrents in the team can safely emerge. Sometimes referred to as a 'holding space' for the emotional intensity of the group and their situation, this enables conversations to happen that simply haven't happened before. Teams do not have many such spaces. Meetings often take the form of a series of monologues to be survived, rather than providing a space where people can share the intensity and complexity of their circumstances. Teams cannot learn or change without dialogue, and without a consciously held container, no dialogue will happen. Instead, people will try to avoid issues, resist what is happening or resort to blame.

As a team coach, much of your initial focus will be on creating such a container. Over time, the container can evolve and deepen and be held by the team rather than by you. The process of building the container starts, as always, with how you are showing up and your mindset. Adopting an 'I'm OK, you're OK, they're OK, we're OK' mindset creates the atmosphere, or 'field', for the work.

Once you are successfully managing your way of being, then draw your focus on to consciously managing the boundaries, as this is essential for creating safety. One way of thinking about boundaries is as a set of norms for how interactions will happen. Norms are patterns of behaviour that naturally develop in teams. Over time, these form into habits until they become behavioural expectations or a social contract. These habits may support or hinder team effectiveness. Norms determine how a team operates, for example how meeting agendas are structured. They shape how people interact with each other. Are they loud, playful and boisterous, or formal and clipped? They determine whether people arrive to meetings on time and get straight down to business, or whether lateness is normal alongside a good deal of social banter before getting to task. They define how decisions are made and how people are held to account. They also deal with how the team deals with conflict – or doesn't.

Teams cannot NOT form norms!

So intelligent teams will form them consciously and intentionally.

Sometimes referred to as 'ground rules', 'golden rules' or 'operating principles', norms can be formed into a set of agreements that guide team expectations and behaviour. Well-formed norms have many positive benefits, such as providing a sense of control and security in the team, as well as a sense of responsibility, accountability and trust.

By way of example, I often observe top teams during their normal routine meetings, and it is common to find a team member presenting to the tops of their colleagues' heads, as they are busy reading papers or making notes while the presenter is speaking. Have you ever tried speaking with conviction or had a game-changing conversation when no one is looking at you? A useful ground rule might be for team members to be conscious of looking up to engage in the conversation that is happening before them.

Visit the book website for some great sets of norms that you can share with teams.

However, every team operates in a different culture and context, and this will inform the norms that are likely to be the most effective for the team you are coaching. So, invite the team to explore and develop norms and practices that transform unhelpful habits into helpful ones.

While not exhaustive, here is a list of areas to explore with teams:

- ➤ What structure of team meetings will best serve you?
  - ➤ How will agendas be formed?
  - ➤ Who will lead the meeting?
  - ➤ How much time will we allow for debate?
  - ➤ Who will record discussions and decisions?
  - ➤ How will information be cascaded?
- ➤ What are your expectations of each other at meetings?
  - ➤ Is it acceptable to miss meetings?
  - ➤ If so, can another representative stand in?
  - ➤ How will you encourage participation?
  - ➤ How will you ensure dialogue is meaningful and useful?
  - ➤ How will you enforce norms and standards?
- ➤ How will you discuss and debate items?
  - ➤ How will decisions be made?
  - ➤ How will follow-up actions be tracked?
  - ➤ How will you hold each other to account for executing decisions?
- ➤ What sparks conflict?
  - ➤ How will it be worked with?
  - ➤ How do we agree to be with each other in times of conflict?
  - ➤ How do we deal with mistakes?

There is one thing in common across all high-performing teams: they have developed group norms that create a sense of togetherness while also encouraging people to take risks.

Check-ins

> Most individuals can't seem to recognize the undercurrents beneath the surface of their conversations, undercurrents that can bring people together or tear them apart.
> – WILLIAM ISAACS (1999)

A check-in is one of the simplest practices of team coaching, inviting people, one-by-one, to say a few words about what thoughts or feelings are moving them in the moment. The beauty of check-ins is that they call on our humanity, inviting us to speak to our own experience and to what matters most to us. The opportunity is to slow the pace, in order to connect, reflect and to be heard. Check-ins often begin the process of surfacing the undercurrents that exist beneath the surface of the conversation, as these often contain crucial information for any subsequent team dialogue.

While some practitioners advocate for specific check-in processes, such as thinking rounds, round robins or using 'talking sticks' or other artefacts, I personally find it best to keep the process very simple and with few instructions other than to listen and be present. How you hold the space and your own presence can be far more impactful than a prescribed process. Once the team experiences the art of checking in together, they rarely go back. As Peter Senge says, 'Once awakened, people do not go back to sleep.'

For your own sanity and protection, it is worthwhile noting that you cannot create psychological safety in all contexts and conditions. Many coaches, myself included, passionately believe in human potential, and they are deeply motivated to make the world a better place. But some workplaces are toxic – characterised by drama, in-fighting, politics and personal battles. They are often the result of corruption and leaders who are motivated by personal power, status and wealth, and who are prepared to use unethical and/or illegal means to achieve their aims. Watch out for any fantasies you may have of being able to fix what is deeply broken. You may be a great coach, but you don't have the power to change a whole culture alone, and you can get hurt – feeling like a failure, becoming self-critical, losing confidence – by kidding yourself that you can achieve the unachievable. The context that a team sits within configures what is possible, so pay attention to the context as well as the team.

See Chapter 12 for more on check-ins.

Competency 4: Effective Relating

How we think does affect how we talk. And how we talk together definitely determines our effectiveness.

– WILLIAM ISAACS (1999)

Today's problems are too complex to be managed by one person alone. We need collective intelligence to solve them. *Effective relating* is therefore essential for the breakthroughs that are necessary for organisations to thrive in this world of turbulence and interdependence. It requires a demonstrable commitment to the relationship, which is something rarely considered or expressed in organisational life, and the art of dialogue which seems to have been all but lost in our modern culture.

This goes beyond listening into thinking and reflecting together, towards building on ideas to arrive at better outcomes. As a team coach, you can actively role-model constructive conflict by demonstrating how to differ in a way that develops mutual understanding, grows respect and develops relationships.

Team coaching is inherently relational. You get into a real relationship with the team, negotiating different perspectives within the team and between the team and yourself. You create greater trust and safety over time by holding a space where differences can be openly expressed and explored. This means being willing to show how the team is impacting you, being respectful and authentic in your response.

Being-with, rather than *doing-to*, is the essence of a relational approach. This doesn't arise from an agenda item or a set of objectives to achieve, yet it is fundamental to optimal team functioning. Taking a relational approach requires wholehearted commitment to the relationship and to dialogue. Dialogue is an emergent form of communication, and it cannot be planned or facilitated. Our commitment to relationship is therefore more of a stance than a technique or methodology. It is the very attitude or mindset that shapes how we relate to others.

We define the competency *effective relating* as 'the ability to be open, in the moment, actively available and responsive'.

Open: this is the opposite of closed. In relational terms, if we are closed, we are putting up a barrier with the aim of preventing anyone or anything from impacting us. Therefore, openness requires us to take off our armour and allow ourselves to be vulnerable. From this place, we can engage in open, meaningful and flexible communication.

In the moment: relationships are formed through moment-by-moment interaction. We learn about each other and life through our relationships. We show up authentically in each moment, open to others and to our differences.

Actively available and responsive: there can be nothing more deadening than speaking your truth only to be met by a poker-faced, deadpan expression. As a team coach, your energetic availability and responsiveness to others is the key that opens the door to the team's development.

It was mid-afternoon, and the team had spent several hours debating their priorities. The conversation seemed to be spinning around in circles. Each of the nine executives was eager to advocate their own view on the priorities, yet with no connection to what the previous speaker was saying. Some were getting more airtime through sheer force of argument, and others had emotionally checked out. Energy was getting low, and irritation was creeping in.

I remained alert yet calm, connecting with others and the situation around me, 'sitting in the fire'. After a few minutes more, I intervened: 'I sense some stuckness – what is happening for each of you right now? Can we stay with this for a moment?'

After an uncomfortable silence, one team member spoke up, reporting he felt frustrated (several others nodded agreement). Another said she'd mentally checked out ten minutes ago. Another team member took a risk, saying 'This is normal, we go round and round in circles until we're out of time.'

I replied, 'I imagine that feels very frustrating. I wonder what it would be like to bring nine brilliant minds into alignment?' I invited them to create an experiment to try this out.

They spent the next 15 minutes discussing what they could do differently. The experiment they created was for one person to facilitate the team through giving each person the space to share their perspective, and others in the team would listen and enquire without advocating a view. They would then have a round of seeking to build the ideas, and then a final round seeking a conclusion.

We experimented with this process, pausing several times to check progress and to tweak the process. The energy shifted to upbeat and engaged, and everyone participated. I offered encouragement, noticing what appeared to be working well along the way. The session ended with a review of the team's learning and a commitment to taking this learning into their regular meetings.

Hopefully you can see that an empathic response can help to give voice to any frustrations and invites the team to create new options and ways of working together.

Working through differences

A team's strength comes from its diverse views. However, while diversity can improve the necessary debate that drives decision-making, when it is time to make decisions, teams often struggle to integrate different and seemingly opposite perspectives, as illustrated above.

Team members often have different perspectives on the same situation because they have different roles and therefore have different agendas and information. How we see things depends on where we are looking from.

Imagine how much more productivity would be gained in teams across the world if their collective intelligence could be harnessed. Team coaches have an important role to play in this by creating a space for the team to pause and to explore how they can make collective sense out of multiple perspectives that seem at odds with each other.

Often if you observe a team in action, you'll notice that people frequently go straight to positions or solutions that they advocate. Instead, invite the team to dig deeper to understand each other's interests rather than their positions. Interests are the underlying needs or concerns that people use to generate their positions.

To illustrate with a simple example, if two people are in a meeting and one says they want to break for 15 minutes and the other wants to continue until a decision is made, those are positions. If you ask 'What leads you to want a break?', one might say that they are tired and need to refresh themselves to continue the conversation. If you then ask the other 'What leads you to want to continue until a decision is made?', they might say it's because they are concerned that they'll run out of time and won't get to a decision. Now we understand the different interests, and we can ask them 'How can you solve this in a way that meets both your interests?'

Coaching pairs

Many team coaches prefer working in coaching pairs. When working as a pair, you have a real opportunity to model effective relating. Demonstrating an effective ongoing working relationship between the coaching pair can greatly contribute to the team's learning. Whereas facilitators and trainers often divide up the leadership of sections of an agenda, the coaching pair works side by side. They therefore need to learn and develop sophisticated skills in reading each other and trusting when to lead and when to follow in the relationship dance. They listen to each other, openly building on each other's ideas and, when their perspectives differ, they demonstrate using curiosity and enquiry transparently to inform their decision-making.

Reflection time

Psychological safety is essential for a team to risk trying out new ways of working and is therefore a pre-condition for learning and change. Trust is an individual phenomenon, i.e. it exists in a team member whereas psychological safety occurs between team members. Ask yourself:

➤ What do I need to be able to trust X (particular team member)?

➤ What would erode this trust?

➤ How can I contribute to developing a more trust-based relationship with X (team member)?

➤ What do I need (make it personal) for it to be safe in this team (as a member or team coach)?

➤ What would erode this psychological safety and what would be the signs of this?

➤ If I observe these signs, what action will I take?

➤ How can I contribute to building psychological safety in a team and what do I need from others to do this?

What have you learned about effective relating and creating psychological safety and trust, and how will you integrate this learning into your team coaching approach?

'It takes two to tango' as the saying goes and this is no truer than in a relational approach to team coaching. By their very nature, relationships are formed between more than one person and often multiple people if a team is made up of several members. Relationships can therefore be co-created. This does not come easily to many teams and so team coaches can demonstrate this through the effective relating competency.

Try the following to develop your effective relating competence. Think about significant relationships in your life (at work and outside of work). Ask yourself:

➤ How do you 'do' relationships? Whom do you easily relate to? Who less easily? What is it about this person(s), real or perceived, that contributes to a closer bond or greater distance between you?

➤ Who do you choose to actively avoid and why? This might reveal some disowned parts of you (your shadow) that you project onto and then see in others. Learn to acknowledge and fall in love with your disowned self. It might also increase your awareness of others you might unconsciously avoid (e.g. pay less attention to) when team coaching!

➤ What is it like being with yourself? Can you become more comfortable with this and accept yourself? When are you more/less attuned with yourself? What triggers this?

➤ What is it like being with others? Can you become more comfortable with this and accept others to be able to relate to them? When are you more/less attuned with others? What triggers this?

➤ How do you build relationships? How do you maintain them? What do you do/not do?

Remember, relationships are forged (strengthened) through heat and pressure. Has a team experienced enough heat to forge strong relationships? What would happen if you were to turn up the heat while team coaching?

9 Fostering Effective Communication

> In almost every setting where practices of dialogue have become embedded and part of everyday routines, the ensuing changes have become irreversible, as near as I can tell.
>
> – PETER SENGE, in foreword to Isaacs (1999)

Effective communication is the linchpin of all human interaction and is an active and skilful procedure. In teams, it is the fundamental currency of exchange, and it shapes every thought, deed and action – for better or worse. Without communication, there is no teamwork.

Therefore, the three competencies for Fostering Effective Communication are as essential for teams to master as they are for team coaches. They are: *direct communication*, *powerful questioning* and *active listening*.

Competency 5: Active Listening

I never saw an instance of one or two disputants convincing the other by arguments.

– THOMAS JEFFERSON, Letters

At TCS, we describe *active listening* as 'the ability to listen deeply to team members, the team and the voice of the system, in the context of the client's desired change'. Both words 'active' and 'listening' are vital. Listening is not a passive endeavour, it is dynamic and collaborative. As a team coach, you create a space where listening can occur. You listen cumulatively from session to session and throughout each individual session. You listen for the team's aspirations, goals, values and beliefs. You summarise what has been said to increase understanding and enable the team to hear each other. As sensitive areas are raised, you encourage people to express their issues, concerns and needs, and reinforce any thoughts and feelings they express.

The role of the coach is to listen without criticism or trying to 'fix' any perceived problem. This enables the team to vent their feelings without judgement or attachment and to feel accepted, be more present and to move on. As they explore their concerns, support team members to actually listen to and hear each other, and to build on ideas and suggestions.

Listening without an agenda is listening with humility. Instead of interpreting what we see through our own mental models, we need to distinguish between the conclusions we are making about an experience and the experience itself. We all jump to conclusions, but our conclusions are not reality. Isaacs (1999) says, 'Listening requires that we not only hear the words, but also embrace, accept, and gradually let go of our own inner clamoring.' This means listening to others as well as to ourselves and our own reactions. Listen in a way that allows the system to speak to you. Slow the process down to hear between the words, tone of voice and body language of the team. Listen to both the words and the silence between words, communicated through body language and a felt sense. Pay attention when something meaningful is said, when new learning and capability is found, and when the team discovers a powerful sense of insight, identity and team spirit.

Listen for the team's voice and what is wanting to be spoken at the collective level. As with music, you can discern any one note, or you can tune into whole composition and its melody. Everything is inter-connected; each phrase in music contains information about the whole symphony. Listen to the wider dimensions surrounding the team, opening the door to greater connection with the emerging needs of stakeholders and the world. Listening in this way helps people and teams to resolve differences and to become more aware of their participation in a much wider whole.

I asked if they were ready to begin our session and then invited the CEO to begin checking-in. He started talking passionately about the growth of the brand and opportunities.

I noticed the FD crossed his arms, was frowning and was looking down, fiddling with his pen. As the CEO continued, I started to feel a knot in my stomach, and sensed something was up. I asked to pause and said, 'As I sit with you here, I am feeling uneasy. I am curious, what are you experiencing right now?' (I had been coaching the team for a while and they were used to me asking this question.)

The sales director said, 'It's amazing, I really think we're on the tipping point.'

I noticed the FD stiffen. I asked him, 'I noticed you sat more upright and folded your arms more tightly. I'm curious, what is happening for you?' He said, 'I'm just worried that we're ignoring the fact that we need to make a profit. Sales are great but without profit, we're screwed.'

After a long silence, the CEO spoke, his tone lower and his energy flatter than before. 'Look, I don't want to worry you all as we're so close to success, but if we don't raise more cash then we'll be out of business in two months at the current burn rate.' I sat silently, holding the space. The tension was palpable and it seemed like we were all holding our breath. They had worked hard and achieved so much and now they were on the brink of failure.

I said, 'I heard you [CEO] say that you didn't want to worry the team and I am curious about the team members' responses to that.' The ops director started to respond, looking to me as he spoke. I quickly held up my hand, saying 'I invite you to speak directly to the CEO' (keeping them connected with each other rather than with me). He turned to the CEO. 'I think we all figured that might be the case, but we didn't want to burst your bubble by speaking about it as I'm not sure we can do much about it.'

Active listening begins with becoming conscious of how you are listening. Listen to yourself and your own reactions, asking yourself what you are feeling now. By connecting with your feelings, you are connecting to the heart of the collective experience. As a result, the team feels acceptance, trust and openness, and responds accordingly. These are all clues that the masterful coach uses to fully understand the essence of the team's collective spirit.

In real coaching stories, it is impossible to separate *active listening* from powerful questions, as well as other competencies and metaskills in action. For example, you may get a sense that I was using the metaskills of presence and use of self.

Competency 6: Powerful Questioning

> The important and difficult job is never to find the right answers. It is to find the right question.
>
> – PETER DRUCKER, *The Practice of Management*

Experienced coaches know that asking rather than telling is central to their work. Telling stops people from having to think. Asking questions causes them to think for themselves. Edgar Schein (2013) describes 'humble inquiry' as 'the fine art of drawing someone out, of asking questions to which you do not already know the answer, of building a relationship based on curiosity and interest in the other person'. Great questions generate creative thinking and catalyse breakthroughs. They unlock the imagination and invite exploration, reflection and discovery.

When used in team coaching, powerful questions focus attention and create clarity. They generate awareness and shift responsibility to the team. Powerful questions can help a team to shape their identity and strengthen their belief and motivation. They serve to clarify the team's collective endeavour and shift a disjointed team into alignment, evoking the collective versus the individual.

Most importantly for ongoing team performance and wellbeing, they help the team to learn, grow and achieve success.

Powerful questions in team coaching

A consultant asks questions to gather information, diagnose and make recommendations. The consultant has the expertise, and the client is the beneficiary. In contrast, as a team coach you trust the team has the answers they need. The purpose of your questions is to create awareness, insight, options and change. By finding answers and solutions, the team becomes more energised and resourceful, and therefore more likely to own the results. The most effective team coaches have 'be curious' as a core mantra in their stance, and curiosity needs questions that get the team looking for answers.

So, what are the specific considerations for using powerful questions with teams? A key principle is that coaching questions follow the team's interests and agenda, not that of the coach, because when the coach leads the focus of the questions, they are in danger of directing the team, reducing its collective responsibility. But, following the team's lead can be a challenge as different team members often try to row the conversational boat in different directions, leaving the team spinning around in circles. Team coaches therefore need creative ways to get the team to focus in one direction for long enough to get some meaningful work done.

Generating a collective figure of interest

A key concept in gestalt psychology is *figure–ground* (see Chapter 12), a natural human perceptual process that refers to what we pay attention to and what we don't. The 'figure of interest' is the focus of our attention and meaning-making; the 'ground' is everything else that is in the background.

Teams are almost always navigating between the competing figures of interest of its members, unless a crisis serves to focus the collective mind. So, the art of team coaching is identifying a collective figure that can be explored by the whole team. Here are some questions that can serve to shift a team from divergence to a common focus:

➤ **What is the common denominator in all your apparently different views?**

➤ **If the team was an entity in its own right, what would it say?**

➤ **What is it that people together are trying to say here?**

These questions seek to evoke an emerging story or voice that captures more than what any one person is saying – the voice of the team.

Finding the team's purpose

For a group of individuals to form as a team, there needs to be a common purpose. A clear, challenging and consequential team purpose drives the inspiration, commitment and collaboration required to achieve remarkable results as a team. In the absence of a compelling collective purpose, team members usually focus their energy and time on achieving outcomes for their service or function, or for themselves.

A team's purpose can be defined by the team leader, the team's stakeholders, team members or a combination of all of these. There are many questions coaches can ask to clarify the team's purpose, such as:

➤ Why does your team exist?

➤ What is the real added value you bring as a team?

➤ What is the job of the team?

➤ What benefit will you bring to the company and the world?

➤ What work does this team need to do together as a team?

Drawing on the collective wisdom of the team

So far, I have described the coach's role in asking questions. At the 2017 ICF Converge conference in Washington, MIT Leadership Centre executive director Hal Gregersen made a brilliant keynote speech where he challenged us to brainstorm for questions, not answers. The audience was invited to engage in a short six-minute process called a 'question burst' that we could apply to solving our own problems, as well as with our coaching clients. I have since tried this approach in team coaching with great results. It takes just four simple steps:

1. Set the stage: select a challenge that the team cares deeply about.

2. Brainstorm the questions: invite the team to spend four minutes generating as many questions about the challenge as they can.

3. Identify a quest: invite them to study the questions, select a few 'catalytic' questions from the list and expand these into their own sets of related or follow-on questions. By deepening understanding around why a question matters and exploring the obstacles in addressing it, you increase the resolve and ability to do something about it.

4. Commit to it: ask them to commit to pursuing at least one new pathway they have glimpsed and do what it takes to get the job done. Encourage them to avoid taking the comfortable or easy route and instead, to focus on what will get the problem solved.

Tips:

➤ Go for at least 15–20 questions in the time allotted.

➤ Don't answer any of the questions or explain why you're asking the question.

➤ Catalytic questions are the ones that hold the most potential for disrupting the status quo.

To read more about question bursts and this approach, see Gregersen's work (2018a,b).

While I have given some example questions here, truly powerful coaching questions emerge spontaneously during the team coaching, often even taking you by surprise. This requires a strong team–coach relationship founded on *psychological safety and trust*. When you are fully present to STS (self, team and situation), powerful questions will simply come to you.

 Visit the book website for a handout on powerful questions in team coaching.

Competency 7: Direct Communication

When your heart and mind are clear, you are able to speak simply and directly. If you are cluttered with 'should', 'what ifs', fear, emotion, or judgement, your message is cloudy.

– MARION FRANKLIN, 'Life's Little Lessons' newsletter

Asking questions is potentially very powerful, but coaches often need other skills to be impactful in team coaching. *Direct communication* is a business-critical skill for team coaches as it is about seeing other perspectives and providing feedback and challenge.

Teams are messy, and information flows across multiple sources and at multiple levels. People often say what they don't mean and struggle to say what they do mean. Useful ideas get lost in translation, and the person who shouts the loudest gets heard. People are masters of indirect communication, acting out rather than directly expressing a view or a concern. This can lead to false assumptions and misunderstandings, conflict and loss of trust. Because of this, *direct communication* is one of the most important competencies.

At TCS, we define *direct communication* as 'the ability to communicate clearly and directly in coaching interactions'. The skill involves:

1. Clearly stating coaching objectives, session topic and the purpose of exercises.

2. Using language that is appropriate and respectful in order to illuminate the team's process or to illustrate a point.

3. Being clear, articulate and direct in sharing and providing feedback.

4. Reframing to help understand other perspectives.

5. Naming and challenging assumptions and limiting beliefs.

> It was the autumn of 2020. Ground down by months of trying to lead through repeated cycles of lockdown, staff engagement scores had plummeted. As an organisation that took pride in being on the 'Best companies to work for' list, the senior team were alarmed by these scores. They acknowledged that, since lockdown, they had cancelled their annual staff conference and 'town hall' meetings. Diving deeper into their reality, they realised that their meetings, all conducted virtually, had become very transactional as they focused on getting tasks done as efficiently as possible. When asked 'What are the possibilities?', they responded that they would need to wait to improve staff engagement until lockdown was over and they could meet their staff in person. I said, 'An engaged workforce will help you to navigate this crisis.' This was enough to open up new possibilities and, a week later, the senior team hosted an organisation-wide virtual staff meeting to reconnect, listen and offer reassurance.

As you can see *direct communication* is a laser-guided statement – 'An engaged workforce will help you to navigate this crisis' – not a question. It may be followed by a question, but make sure the statement has time to land.

It also includes 'reframing' to help the team to look at the situation from a different perspective. This can include direct messages, reflections and observations or metaphors, as these can be very effective at cutting to the chase, such as 'It's like a puzzle and you are each looking at individual pieces. How can you bring all the pieces together to form one picture?' Or, you might say, 'This team is like a skein of flying geese, taking it in turns to be the leader' to highlight the team's progress in sharing leadership.

A final word: remember when using *direct communication* with a team, you are role-modelling a skill that is incredibly valuable for team members to master as well. So it helps to practise this competence with fellow coaches so that it becomes second nature and can be applied with ease.

Reflection time

The currency of any relationship is the ability to communicate – to both listen and speak – and this chapter explains both.

While both active listening and direct communication apply to the team coach, they can also relate to a team too. In other words, they are competencies for the coach to demonstrate and also for the coach to encourage in a team, thus the coach 'fosters' effective communication in a team. Both are developable skills for the team coach.

Try this activity to develop your active listening:

➤ Reflect upon your most recent work with groups and teams.

➤ Who did you listen to – the whole team as an intact entity or individual team members – or both? How do you listen to the 'voice of the team' and how does a team hear this?

➤ What were you listening for? You likely have patterns in your listening habits. After each team coaching session, make some brief notes about what you heard. Compare them across sessions and between different teams. What patterns can you observe?

➤ What are you paying attention to? How much of your attention is any particular person and/or topic taking? Given this focus, what might we be paying little or no attention to?

➤ What are your favourite and least favourite things to listen out for?

➤ Check the focus of what you listened for and heard with a co- or paired team coach. The chances are you listened to and heard different things. How can you widen your collective listening radar? How can you fill any gaps in your collective listening?

'Direct communication' is harder than it sounds. To develop this competency, try:

➤ Laser focus – practise being precise in your communication. Avoid jargon and complex words. Keep any instructions short. Check the team's understanding. Notice the effect of this sharper focus on a team.

➤ Brevity – practise using as few words as possible, keeping your language simple and straightforward. Notice the effect of this brevity on a team.

What have you learned about the active listening and direct communications competencies, and how will you integrate this learning into your team coaching practice?

How do/will you develop a team's active listening and direct communications capabilities?

10 Working with Systems & Dynamics

We can't impose our will upon a system.

We can listen to what the system tells us...

We can't control systems or figure them out.

But we can dance with them!

– DONELLA MEADOWS (2008)

The air changes and a slight breeze ruffles the leaves. Clouds are amassing and you sense rain is coming. First a drop, then a cascade, running down the street and into the drains. The rainstorm continues for hours, and then days. The river that runs through your hometown floods, causing houses to be evacuated and people to disperse to stay with friends and family elsewhere. As Senge (2006) says, 'You can only understand the system of a rainstorm by contemplating the whole, not any individual part of the pattern.'

Barry Oshry (2007) made a simple observation about systems. In multiple organisations, regardless of geography, industry or sector, he noticed the same self-limiting patterns of behaviour. When problems were identified, the organisation sought the culprits and fired, shuffled or changed the players. But the problem didn't go away; the same issues kept coming back. He realised that most problems in organisations were not personal, they were systemic. The path to success was not in changing the players but in 'seeing the system' – the interconnected patterns – and working on the underlying issues.

> Systems thinking is a discipline for seeing wholes. It is a framework for seeing interrelationships rather than things, for seeing 'patterns of change' rather than static 'snapshots'.
>
> – PETER SENGE (2006)

As much as we might try, systems are not controllable; they are non-linear, self-organising and unpredictable. We might dream about the future and make plans that we expect to be fully realisable. This may work when we set out to bake a cake, but setting out to make a complex system do what you want it to do is a fantasy. You can't control systems, but you can dance with them.

Dancing with the system means envisioning rather than predicting; designing rather than planning; expecting change and flexing and adapting to what is emerging; learning as we go. It means seeing the system, listening to the system, being influenced by the system. Notice how the system behaves and the patterns that emerge within the team and between the team and other teams, and in the wider organisation. Notice what is occurring in the world at political, social, economic and psychological levels. Listen to the wisdom the system has to share with you.

What do we mean by 'systemic'?

The term 'systemic' has become very popular in the field of team coaching, offered in the form of specific activities, such as 360° interviews or 'constellations'. Sometimes, however, these processes are abstracted from the broader principles that inform all systemic approaches.

In team coaching we are focusing on relationship systems – meaning any group of people who share a common identity or purpose. A group is a discrete entity with its own personality and culture created through its history by the relationships that exist between members and those it interacts with. It is like a marriage, where both people are separate 'I's and the marriage is the 'we' of the relationship. A healthy marriage supports the 'we'.

When you see the team as a relational system, it becomes more than the sum of its parts, an entity in its own right. A team entity has its own identity, purpose, values, goals, network of relationships, needs and challenges. By relating to a team as a relational system, you are focusing on the 'power and potential of we', channelling the collective intelligence and energy of the team.

'The word "systemic" is being appropriated by different authors to mean quite different things.' (Lawrence, 2021) As coaches, we need to understand how we think about systems, as the way we see a system will shape our methodology and how we coach the team. I am not going to compare the different systemic approaches here but recommend reading Lawrence's four-part series of white papers on 'The Systemic Coach' to learn more.

Visit the book website to download Lawrence's white papers.

As well as thinking about interconnectedness and patterns, working with systems and dynamics also means looking at how culture and context are creating conditions that define how the team is thinking and behaving. If you join our webinars or courses on team coaching, you'll often hear us say 'context configures the field', or 'context shapes what is possible'.

In the cluster 'Working with Systems & Dynamics', there are three competencies: *focus on relationships in the system (shortened to 'relationship systems' in the diagram); engage with the wider context and stakeholder expectations (wider context and stakeholders)* and *working with power and authority (power and authority).*

Competency 8: Focus on Relationships in the System

Individually, we are one drop. Together, we are an ocean.

– RYUNOSUKE SATORO

We describe this competency as 'the ability to serve the team collectively, in a system, while acknowledging the interests, strengths, values and needs of the individual'.

This is about assisting the team to form its identity consciously and to make sense of the intricate nature of the relationships between members. It involves noticing patterns, observing roles that are playing out, recognising power dynamics and surfacing what has so far been unspoken. It is also about intervening at the appropriate level of the system.

Levels of the system

Any organisational system has many levels – individual, dyad, subgroup, team, inter-team, organisation, wider stakeholder system or beyond.

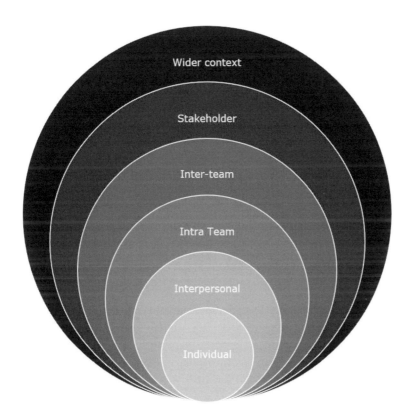

Levels of a system

A key question to ask is, 'Who do conversations need to be between?'

Considering this question, read these example situations:

1. A new team needs to accelerate the process of forming. They want to get to know each other, to understand each other's strengths and weaknesses, and to work on a team charter.

2. Two team members are subsumed by conflict. Activities are driven by the more assertive individual and the quieter one has almost 'disappeared'. The rest of the team have become bystanders, walking on eggshells around the conflict.

3. The marketing team are underperforming and most of their projects are delayed or not having the desired impact. They blame the products team, claiming that they focus on their own pet projects rather than on those needed by the business.

4. Post merger, the organisation is struggling to materialise any gains due to a clash of cultures and tribal warfare.

5. A publishing organisation is facing an existential crisis. Consumers are no longer buying newspapers and profits are falling at a pace. The senior team are looking for a coach to support them to re-imagine the organisation.

 Visit the book website to see a handout with my responses.

Reconnect what has become disconnected

In the frenetic pace of everyday business life, it is easy for a team to become disconnected. Instead of operating as an effective whole, the team fragments with each team member focusing their time and energy on their own function, division or individual goals or interests. Gone is the sense of 'we' and we now have a collection of 'I's. A team can also disconnect from the wider system, for example the senior team whose decisions are not aligned with their board of trustees, or an IT team who are unaware of their internal stakeholders' perception and needs.

Successful teams notice when this happens and take steps to remedy it by shifting their focus to their interconnected and interdependent relationships. They then seek to 'join the dots', reconnecting what has become disconnected.

Team coaching provides a space where everyone has a voice and is heard. It also provides a space for team members to come together around their greater purpose and to process any difficult conversations that have been avoided. When people feel listened to and understood, and when they see how they contribute to the collective whole, a dynamic shift happens towards collaboration.

To reconnect what has become disconnected, coach the team to:

➤ make sure everyone is crystal clear on the team's purpose and goals, and their role in achieving these

➤ identify interdependencies and opportunities for collaboration

➤ surface barriers to collaboration and move towards alignment

➤ become aware of disconnects and develop their capacity to reconnect

➤ take regular pauses for team dialogue, supporting collective awareness-raising, meaning-making and collaborative decision-making.

Triangulation

As a team coach, you potentially get told a lot about individuals, the leader and various dynamics between team members. Triangulation occurs in teams when person A talks about person B to person C – usually in the form of a complaint or criticism. This feeds fragmentation, which can be transformed into connection by supporting people to have open and honest conversations with each other about points of conflict, expressing their feelings and making requests of each other.

Introduce the concept of triangulation to teams and ask about the effect it has on them, the team and their organisation. You can then explore alternatives to shift behaviour from triangulation towards healthy communication and constructive conflict. For example:

'Imagine you just left a team meeting and you are frustrated. You go for a coffee with one of your fellow team members. What do you say?'

Perhaps followed by: 'What might be stopping you from having this conversation with the team?'

Often their concerns stem from a lack of *psychological safety and trust*.

Experiment with collapsing the triangle in team coaching. Here are some examples:

➤ 'Mike, would you be willing to say that to Jo directly? If so, how about we rehearse it?'

➤ 'How can I support you so you can voice your concerns?'

➤ 'What can you accomplish together?'

➤ [To A] 'What is important to B about this topic? What is your stand on the topic?'

➤ 'What does the team need from you as a pair?'

Sometimes people have not yet developed the skills of *direct communication* that we discussed in the previous chapter. This may present an opportunity to practise difficult conversations with a team to build up their *direct communication* muscle. In this way, they can find a common language and approach that is acceptable to them as a team.

Leverage individual strengths in service of the team's effectiveness

Rarely do I encounter a team that is truly leveraging the strengths of the individuals in the team to enable the team entity to be more effective. Yet doing so can free up teams when they get stuck, increase energy, engagement and a sense of belonging, and improve the team's effectiveness.

David, the CEO, an evangelist by nature, was extremely skilful at rallying the team's energy around their collective purpose. Facilitative by style, he was brilliant at asking open questions, generating rich debate and building trust. However, he often failed to ensure that decisions were clear and understood or to check that the team was aligned.

As I observed the team in action, my attention was drawn to Richard, who naturally sought to bring clarity to the conversation. He was articulate, concise and he took notes. However, his strengths weren't being employed in service of the team. I shared this observation and asked the team how his strengths could better serve the team. The CEO had assumed it was his role to facilitate the team meeting, including setting the agenda, driving the energy, opening up the debate and wrapping up. He hadn't considered asking other team members to contribute towards running the meeting. Once Richard was empowered to assume the role of clarifying decisions and testing for alignment, team meetings instantly became more productive. Eventually, responsibility for many of the team's processes were distributed across the members, leaving the CEO to play to his strengths.

What questions can you use to explore the team's strengths and the role they can contribute towards greater team effectiveness? Here are some of mine:

➤ **What strengths do you appreciate in each other?**

➤ **What do you bring to the team?**

➤ **Which strengths do you individually have, but could leverage more?**

➤ **What informal roles do you need in the team to be effective?**

➤ **Who could contribute to these roles?**

When I say an 'informal role', I mean a part an individual plays in the team, such as coordinator, devil's advocate, expert, clarity-seeker, ideas generator, organiser, nurturer, etc.

Competency 9: Engage with the Wider Context and Stakeholder Expectations

> There is a deep interconnectedness of all life on earth, from the tiniest organisms, to the largest ecosystems, and absolutely between each person.

– BRYANT MCGILL, *Voice of Reason*

No team is an island. Organisations are like webs of teams. Each team entity has its own identity, purpose and goals, which need to contribute to the overall purpose and vision of the business. They also need to collaborate with other teams. For example, in an electrical goods manufacturer, the products team needs to ensure that the items they design match customers' needs, so they interface with sales and customer service teams. Marketing needs to promote the products, so they need the products team to be clear on the spec and the benefits. IT provides the online platform for sales and marketing and for the administration of the business, so more interfaces, and so on. Each interfacing team is a 'stakeholder group'.

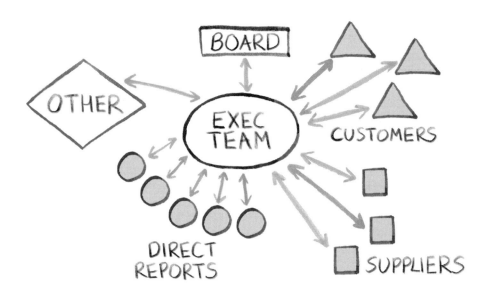

Team stakeholders

The board of the organisation has set priorities to improve the quality of their products and their speed to market; it is also a stakeholder, along with customers, suppliers and staff. Each stakeholder group has expectations of the team you are coaching.

What's more, the team and organisation exist within the wider context of the social, political, economic, environmental and technological system. This wider system has needs which any organisation ignores at its peril. For example, the government's plan to end the sale of new diesel and petrol vehicles by 2035 in the UK will not only influence cars that are being designed and built, it also requires infrastructure changes to provide greater access to electric vehicle charging stations.

In the future, success and sustainability will depend upon a team's capacity to horizon-scan to identify opportunities and challenges and to address these farther upstream than conventional approaches. They will also need to dramatically improve their capacity to engage with and understand their stakeholders, because when companies or teams no longer meet stakeholder needs, they will quickly become irrelevant.

We define the competency of *engaging with the wider system and stakeholder expectations* as 'the ability to work holistically, bringing the system in which the team is operating into the room'. When coaching teams, there are literally hundreds of questions you could ask; these are a few to get started:

➤ Who are the team's stakeholders?

➤ What are their expectations and needs?

➤ What is the quality of the interactions between stakeholders and the team?

➤ Do the team's purpose, goals and priorities align with the rest of the organisation?

➤ How is the wider context changing? What influences are there on the organisation and team? What opportunities do we have to become more relevant in the future?

Beyond using questions, there are many tools and approaches you can use, including stakeholder mapping, empty chair, constellations and stakeholder interviews, to name a few. See Chapter 12 on Frameworks, Tools and Techniques for examples.

Competency 10: Working with Power & Authority

There are a lot of leaders but little leadership out there.

Power is alive in every organisation and team, yet it is rarely talked about and sometimes even considered to be a dirty word. Even in the flattest teams, certain people have more power than others. What creates power is multifaceted; it is derived from title or status, knowledge, skills, experience, relationships and more. It can be used to influence, to engage, to dominate or to control. Power exists, whether we like it or not. Power is a central psychological process going on in groups, whether it is centralised or distributed.

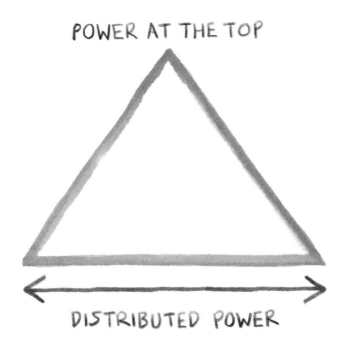

POWER AT THE TOP

DISTRIBUTED POWER

Organisational cultures have quite different beliefs and values around power. Some expect leadership to be top down, and others are more orientated to empowering team members. In leadership development there is a lot of talk about 'empowerment', but sometimes a leader-led team is right for the organisation, and the team. Given this paradigm, in some teams there is a clear 'leader' and in other teams there are leaders.

Leadership has many specific functions in a team, including setting or clarifying the team's purpose and goals, selecting members, establishing reward structures, coordinating tasks and more. Effective teams are transparent about which functions are performed by the team's leader (or leaders) and which by members. For more on this, see 'Authority Matrix' in Chapter 12.

This suggests that coaches should consider what work they do with the leader versus what work they do with the whole team. It is worthwhile examining:

➤ What are the organisation's expectations of the leader?

➤ What are the leader's beliefs around leadership?

➤ How does the leader see their role?

➤ How will decisions be made?

➤ What does the leader get to decide; what do team members get to decide?

At the early stage of a team's development, there is a need for clear leadership. As the team gets more mature, power often becomes more distributed. Leadership is challenging, and sometimes leaders abdicate too much of their authority. Often the team is expecting more direction and clarity from the leader, and the leader is wanting to have more shared leadership. There is a balance between not stepping in when the team need you to or stepping in too much and not giving the team enough room.

Coach leaders to lead their own teams

You can help leaders to develop confidence in leading the team by building rapport with the leader and partnering them. Understand the organisation's expectations of the leader, respecting the authority structure and making it more transparent. Explore the leader's views about their role and how they will use their power, and pay attention to how it's being used in helpful and unhelpful ways. Help them to step up into a leadership role that elicits the best from their team. Leaders become more effective when they sense what is needed, step in and provide the clarity or direction required and, if it isn't needed, they get out of the way.

Coach at the right level

Often it is suggested to coaches that they must coach an intact team to define the team's purpose, but sometimes it is not in their power to set the purpose as it has been decided by commissioners or other stakeholders outside of the team. By way of example, consider a private equity (PE) firm which acquires a business with the aim of doubling it in size in three years, and assembles a senior team to help it achieve this. The desired results are not negotiable, but how the business gets there is the work of the senior team. In this case, getting the stakeholders in the room (the PE firm) to communicate the team's purpose can be enormously helpful.

If the team doesn't have any authority over its own purpose, then don't make the mistake of asking them to co-create it. Instead, work with them to work out how they can deliver on the purpose they have been given.

Coach, know thyself

As a coach, understanding your own relationship with power and authority is essential. Generally, I find that few coaches have given this enough consideration. Some of us have issues with authority, often rooted in our own family or cultural history. Unaware, this can cause us to bypass or undermine the leader. Others have leadership envy and can find themselves leading or competing with the leader. Some have great deference for leaders and can find themselves overly subordinate, and thus losing their capacity to coach the leader. Others admire the hero leader and secretly worship the leader, acting more as the leader's henchman than a coach.

Here are some watch points:

➤ Don't ask the whole team to define their collective purpose, without finding out whether they have the right to determine this.

➤ Don't automatically expect all decisions to be made by consensus without considering the team's authority structure.

➤ Be cautious using voting to get major decisions made. This equalises power, when sometimes a weighted decision method might be more appropriate.

➤ In a team where power is distributed, don't automatically defer all decisions to one leader.

To develop your own capacity to work with power and authority, examine your beliefs around leadership, power and decision-making. Of course, it can be very helpful to work with a colleague or supervisor who can assist you in knowing yourself more deeply.

Reflection time

Teams in organisations don't operate in isolation. They function as a unit and work alongside and with other teams. Collectively, they form a system. This competency cluster, Working with Systems & Dynamics, explores how a team influences and is influenced by the system and context of which it is a part.

Like 'the force' in the Star Wars films, it is all around us and ever present and, although often invisible, it nonetheless has a significant ability to impact a team. As such, it is a key skill for a team coach to see and understand a system more clearly and to help a team do likewise.

Focus on relationships in the system and engaging with the wider context and stakeholders

Interventions with teams are most effective when they are at the correct level of the system. A prerequisite to being able to intervene, then, is to be able to see and make sense of a complex system. Ask yourself:

➤ In what way(s) do you help a system to reveal itself? Which approaches or tools do you use?

➤ How do you engage with the wider context (e.g. other teams; key stakeholders) and enable their needs to be heard by a team?

➤ How do you then seek to understand and make sense of a system?

Think about recent team coaching assignments. What did you notice about:

➤ The flow of the conversation – was it in and out between the team coach and team, or directly between team members and/or the team's leader?

➤ The quality of the team member 'exchanges' (communications)?

➤ How can you encourage more dialogue between team members to improve their relationship strength?

Working with power and authority

➤ As you hear the words 'power' and 'authority', what associations and feelings do these evoke in you?

➤ What is your personal experience of working within a system? What was the culture of this system and which role(s) did you occupy? What power and authority was attached to each role?

➤ As a team coach, in what way(s) do you establish your authority with a team? How might this differ at the start of a team coaching assignment to later in a team coaching journey?

➤ How might you contract around power with the team leader enabling you to intervene with a team while coaching?

➤ What is the significance of power and authority to you and what are the implications for your team coaching practice?

What have you learned about Working with Systems & Dynamics and how will you integrate this learning into your team coaching approach?

11 Facilitating Learning & Growth

> As a team coach, I am an awareness agent rather than a change agent.

Essentially the whole point of team coaching is to cultivate learning and growth. There are many coaches and books talking about 'high performance team coaching', yet this can create confusion about the coach's role. Performance is the domain of the team leader(s) and team. *Facilitating learning and growth* is the domain of the coach, and it starts by *creating awareness*, and flows into *generating results*.

Competency 11: Creating Awareness

Awareness allows us to get outside of our mind

– DAN BRULÉ

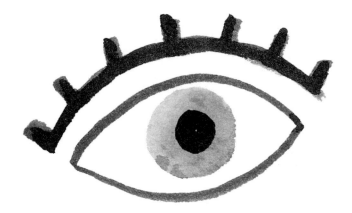

Learning and growth stems from awareness. Einstein famously said, 'No problem can be solved from the same level of consciousness that created it.' We need to cultivate awareness and use this to stimulate change.

In teams, there is no such thing as 'one awareness'; there are multiple awarenesses competing for attention which teams need to learn to synthesise into a connected whole. Heightening a team's awareness and bringing divergence into alignment is an interactive, collaborative and iterative process centred around five key principles:

1. **Create awareness from multiple sources of information and help the team to turn the data into insight.**

2. **Invite the wider contextual and stakeholder perspective into the dialogue.**

3. **Help the team to discover their own values and beliefs.**

4. **Create space for dialogue, staying with what is emerging and supporting collective meaning-making.**

5. **Identify patterns which may be helping or hindering the team's success.**

Create awareness from multiple sources of information, and help the team to turn the data into insight

As already discussed, there are many ways of gathering data to support team coaching, including: team leader and member interviews; stakeholder interviews; the use of team assessments and personality profiles; observing the team in action; and more. It is easy to become overwhelmed in the process of *creating awareness*, so finding effective ways of turning information into insight is essential.

Invite the wider contextual and stakeholder perspective into the dialogue

In Chapter 10, I discussed the different levels of a system where teams can gather data – individual members, the team as an entity, the team's stakeholders and the wider context. Habitually, I find that teams prefer their own perspectives (individual or team level) to those of other stakeholders or the wider context. The team coach therefore often acts as the team's conscience, inviting these voices 'into the room'.

Help the team to discover their own values and beliefs, creating a climate that reflects their desired change

Successful teams have an extraordinary team culture where people are engaged, cooperative and passionate about delivering on the team's purpose. The culture is the *spirit* of the team; it attracts the best talent and compels brilliance. Team culture is the set of fundamental values and beliefs that team members share and that guide their behaviour, such as 'being curious' and 'seeking to understand'. Great teams can articulate their core values and beliefs and they act accordingly. A team that values relationships is likely to build relationships that are strong and lasting; whereas a team that values quality is likely to seek suggestions for improvement. Values can also hinder a team's progress, such as the team which believes that conflict is to be avoided at all costs, rather than seen as essential for creativity and better decision-making.

There are many activities and exercises you can use as a coach to support a team in exploring and clarifying their values. See the book website for examples.

Sadly, it is common for a set of values to become rhetoric rather than practised. It takes conscious intent and discipline to commit to a set of values and live them. It can therefore be helpful for the coach to observe the team's culture in action. Notice how people treat each other, how they behave, how meetings are conducted, how decisions are made and how they conduct their relationships with others. Experience how you are greeted as you enter the building and how you are engaged in your work with the team. Your personal experience of the team, from the initial point of contact, will give you a sense of what they truly value versus what they say they value.

Create space for dialogue, staying with what is emerging and supporting collective meaning-making

> There are no recipes or formulas, no checklists or expert advice that describe 'reality'... We must engage with each other, experiment to find what works for us.

– MARGARET WHEATLEY (2006)

We all know that the world is changing at an incredible pace and the future seems volatile, unpredictable and uncertain. Leadership in today's organisations is like white water rafting in the most extreme rapids, and it requires the very best teamwork where each person brings themselves fully to the table. Team coaching is one of the most effective ways of supporting teams in coping with today's challenges while, at the same time, creating sustainable futures.

A team has a 'collective intelligence' that can only be leveraged when it operates as more than the sum of its parts. Having lots of smart team members doesn't ensure the team will have high collective intelligence. In fact, often it has quite the opposite effect as members compete and vie to be top dog. To generate collective wisdom, teams need diverse thinkers; people who approach problems differently. But diversity alone won't enable them to access the collective wisdom; they need to become excellent collaborators. Team coaching creates space for dialogue and meaning-making, a prerequisite for making better decisions.

> **Meaning-making is the process by which we interpret situations or events in the light of our own experience.**

An experienced team coach will help the team to develop their capacity to be effective in turning their collective meaning making into business-critical intelligence. This becomes a team superpower, helping them to repeatedly win together and safeguarding future success.

Coaches support team meaning-making by:

➤ asking the team to notice, i.e. 'What is going on right now?'

➤ ensuring that all voices are heard and taken into account

➤ encouraging team members to listen to each other, make connections and ask clarifying questions before jumping in with a different view

➤ naming the elephant in the room

➤ sharing their own 'felt sense'.

Identify patterns which may be helping or hindering the team's success

Whenever a group of people engage in working together, they establish ways of relating that become like choreographed dance patterns over time – a systemic dance. These patterns are either productive or counterproductive. They are ultimately creating and reinforcing the team's results.

As a team coach, you observe and raise awareness around the team's interactional patterns. You become curious about whether a pattern is productive and, if not, experiment with more effective ways of working together. Like jazz improvisation, you don't know upfront what patterns will show up and when, so you need to be able to work in the here-and-now rather than relying on pre-prepared exercises that may or may not be helpful.

Competency 12: Generating Results

Alone we can do so little; together we can do so much.

– HELEN KELLER

The purpose of any team is ultimately to generate results. As a team coach, your focus, however, is not on the results themselves; instead it is on what the team needs to learn and how it grows in capability, which in turn produces results. Many team coaches fall into the trap of monitoring the team's performance against their objectives. I argue that it is the role of the team leader and team members to track team progress. If the team coach is also doing this, then it can quickly create role confusion and unclear leadership.

During a supervision group for internal coaches working in a large technology firm, the coaches complained that they felt pulled into holding their coachees accountable for delivery against their performance targets. At the same time, the coachees' managers believed their role was to manage performance and were angry that the coaches were treading on their toes. And the coachees themselves were unclear who they were really reporting to, and who was influencing their performance appraisal ratings. By raising their own awareness around this dynamic, the coaches shifted their focus to re-contracting with their clients around their desired coaching outcomes.

Co-create an effective team coaching plan, leaving responsibility with the team for action and performance

Most one-to-one coaches work to some sort of coaching plan, which details the desired outcomes from the coaching partnership. Even coaches who prefer to work more emergently, with no fixed agenda, recognise the need for an overarching purpose for the team coaching. There is always some reason that a client comes to coaching, and team coaching is no exception.

The questions 'Why team coaching?' and 'Why now?' can be remarkably effective conversation starters. They might be posed to the team leader or HR representative, or to the team as a whole, or to the team's sponsor or stakeholders. The responses to these questions may contribute to desired outcomes from team coaching. To turn this into a plan, follow up questions around what the team needs to learn or change to achieve these desired outcomes are a useful starting point. Nevertheless, rarely are these questions enough as often clients are not clear on what they need to learn or change – they are simply aware that they could be better. For this reason, team coaches often provide a 'discovery phase' at the beginning of a new team coaching programme, the purpose of which is to raise awareness of the opportunities for growth. You can read more about this in Chapter 4.

(As a side note, I advise you to exercise caution in habitually gathering stakeholder input at the early stages of a team coaching programme, as some teams do not have sufficient psychological safety and trust or skills in dialogue to process the data. As a result, the pressure this exerts on a team can cause them to become defensive and even split or fragment. So it is often more productive to focus initially on building the container and their dialogic skills before bringing external data to the table.)

Take responsibility for the coaching process and support the team to stay on track

The coaching process is about partnering the team along a defined team coaching journey and applying the team coaching competencies in service of the team's desired learning and change.

By 'supporting the team to stay on track', we mean on track towards their desired team coaching outcomes. This sounds straightforward enough, but it can be surprisingly difficult to track progress. It is therefore helpful to clarify how the team can track and monitor its progress – I repeat, how the *team* can track its progress. Simple questions work best here, such as:

➤ What are your desired learning and change outcomes?

➤ How will you know when you have achieved this?

➤ How will you track changes along the way?

➤ What will be the indicators of progress along the journey?

➤ What will you see, hear, feel...?

➤ What resources do you need to help you to track progress?

➤ On a scale of 1–10, with 10 being 'on track' and 1 being 'no progress', where are you now?

This can be done through dialogue, or you can get creative and invite the team to produce a team learning and change dashboard – where the team capture their top three to five development goals and track progress against these – or other assessment tool that they can use to measure progress.

Co-creatively explore specific concerns and opportunities that are central to the team's desired coaching outcomes

Whenever there is change, there are concerns and opportunities. It is human nature to both crave change and resist it, often in equal measure. Creating a safe environment where the team can openly discuss and explore any resistance, without criticism or judgement, can be very powerful. We can either choose to work with the opportunities *or* the concerns. Usually, it's better to fully explore one pole at a time, rather than flip-flopping between them, as this can lead to a sense that the opportunities and concerns cancel each other out, resulting in a zero-sum game. Staying with each pole allows it to be explored in greater depth; in this way the team can really engage with an opportunity and what it can mean for the team. This generates excitement and energy. Any concerns can be brought into awareness and worked through in a way that is supportive and enables learning and change to occur.

A senior team wanted to shift from an operational and task focus to being a strategic decision-making team, leading the organisation's ambitious growth plan. They identified opportunities to clarify their vision for the organisation and determined five key, game-changing, strategic goals. Previously, they had dozens of business-as-usual targets that were set departmentally and had not considered having strategic goals that the team would own. While excited and energised by this idea, they wondered why they hadn't done this sooner. They realised they were afraid that they would lose their focus on day-to-day performance. The coach worked with them to explore how they could both lead strategically and maintain performance. Once they acknowledged that it wasn't a case of either/or and that they needed to do both, they moved forward with their plan.

Enable the team to integrate learning, access different resources and celebrate success for future growth

When teams truly integrate learning, they are enhancing their capacities and capabilities to achieve greater success and stakeholder value. This requires a learning culture where the team collectively and intentionally harvests the learning and banks this for future use. Instead of believing they have 'arrived', they celebrate their successes and then set about identifying what they can learn next. Teams with a learning culture believe that they can continually learn and grow more, and view challenges and failures as opportunities to improve.

You can help the team to foster a learning culture by encouraging them to take time to pause, to take stock and to 'slow down to speed up'. Invite team members to share stories of success and to mine for the lessons learned.

Powerful questions are:

➤ What went well?

➤ If we could redo this, what would be even better?

➤ What have you learned?

➤ What new skills and capabilities do you have now as a team?

➤ How can you leverage these further?

➤ If you were to turn this learning into a team superpower, what would you do?

Reflection time

This chapter proposes that a team will change if there is sufficient awareness of the need for change, with the team coach's role being to act as an awareness-raising agent.

Think about teams you have worked with. Ask yourself:

➤ How have you gone about raising awareness in teams? What approaches, methods or tools have you used?

➤ Have you provided information/data (e.g. through the use of psychometric tools) or insights?

➤ How do you help a team (rather than you as team coach) make meaning from data?

➤ What might you do differently as a team coach to support a team to take on the responsibility for sense-making?

➤ How do you stop yourself becoming overloaded and overwhelmed by large amounts of data? How might you support a team to do the same?

➤ How much do you work dynamically 'in the moment' and work with 'what is'? Are you practised at 'naming' dynamics and patterns? Both can help a team make more meaning of what is occurring.

In Chapter 3 we looked at a team coach's beliefs and values. If you skipped this reflective activity or wish to remind yourself of your answers, it would be useful to look at this again. Now ask yourself:

➤ What are your values and beliefs e.g. on teams, change, leadership, etc?

➤ How do you go about identifying a team's values and beliefs?

➤ How do you go about reconciling differences between your values and beliefs as a team coach with those of a team leader and team?

➤ How do you explore the degree to which a team is living and upholding its values?

➤ How do you help teams to reflect and learn?

What have you learned about facilitating learning and growth, and how will you integrate this learning into your team coaching approach?

12 Frameworks, Tools & Techniques

Not I, nor anyone else can travel that road for you.

You must travel it by yourself.

It is not far. It is within reach.

Perhaps you have been on it since you were born, and did not know.

Perhaps it is everywhere – on water and land.

– WALT WHITMAN, *Leaves of Grass*

In this chapter, I offer some conceptual frameworks, tools and techniques that you may find useful as part of your team coaching toolkit. These are in the outer layer of the TCS Team Coaching Wheel as we consider them to be useful and have a place, but they are not essential. The inner core is your philosophy and stance, which shapes your way of being and acting as a team coach. The metaskills provide impact and a here-and-now methodology for change. The team coaching competencies are the skills necessary for any team coach to be effective. So, think of these frameworks, tools and techniques as occasional accompaniments to the main dish – giving your food a lift, adding colour and accentuating certain flavours.

Conceptual frameworks

A defining condition of being human is that we have to understand the meaning of our experience.

– JACK MEZIROW, 'Transformative Learning: Theory to Practice'

We use conceptual frameworks in all walks of life, not just in coaching. They help us to organise ideas and inform the process of meaning-making, which Kegan (1983) describes as the activity of making sense of our experience through discovering and resolving problems. Meaning-making is essential in coaching; it is how we understand and make sense of the circumstances in which we find ourselves. In any group or team, as new things are experienced and integrated, knowledge is actively created and learning occurs.

As a coach, the conceptual frameworks you use help individuals and the team to make sense of their experience, providing a system of organising data into an understandable and workable form. However, they are not neutral; they guide the meaning-maker to view the data from a particular viewpoint. Imagine you are looking at an ocean; the perspective you take will be very different whether you are looking from a dinghy or a giant cruise ship, whether you take an aerial view or are looking up at the surface from the seabed. So, it is important to make sure that your chosen frameworks, tools and techniques are congruent with your philosophy and stance. For example, if your coaching is influenced by solution-focused principles, you may decide to use an Appreciative Inquiry '5 D' framework, inviting the team to make meaning through five aspects of enquiry: define, discover, dream, design and deliver.

Below are some frameworks that many team coaches find useful. They are not a fixed part of my team coaching process; rather, I draw on one when it comes to mind in the light of a situation that is unfolding. Many of the frameworks below can be used in one-to-one coaching as well as team coaching.

The OK Corral

Transactional analysis is founded on the principle that we are all born 'OK' (good and worthy). Franklin Ernst developed this into a matrix which became known as the 'OK Corral'. It is a brilliantly simple model which can help us to understand what happens between people in their encounters with each other.

Each of four life positions holds basic beliefs about self and others, which are used to justify decisions and behaviour and determine how we interact with others. While our 'life position' can be situational, we all have a dominant life position. In all but the healthy 'I am OK, you are OK' position, people are either taking too much or too little responsibility, leading to blame and/or destructive behaviour.

In teams where there is an absence of leadership to provide the necessary structure and support, not-OK-ness can develop. In the vacuum of what people need, a belief that something is wrong can develop, and someone must not be OK. The meaning constructed by each team member will depend on their life position. For example, if 'You are not OK, I am OK', then I am likely to believe that you are to blame.

To develop a sense of OK-ness, team members can monitor their own internal reactions and consider what shift they can make to stay in an OK–OK position.

The OK Corral is a useful model to share with a team to develop greater understanding of why people relate to each other the way they do, and how relationships can be strengthened. You can also experiment with the model by asking the team to discuss a collective topic with each person taking one of the 'Not OK' positions. Pause the discussion after a few minutes and then invite them all to shift to an 'I am OK, you are OK' position and to resume the discussion. This enables the team to experience the different positions in action.

The Six Conditions for Team Effectiveness

Wageman et al. (2008) describe this model in their book *Senior Leadership Teams: What it Takes to Make Them Great*. Their research showed that these six conditions differentiate top performing teams around the world.

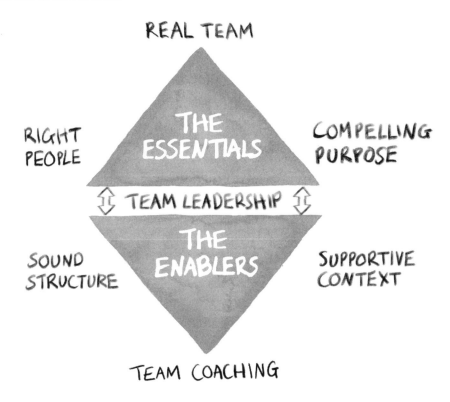

The Six Conditions for Team Effectiveness

There are three *essential* conditions that teams must have to be effective, and three *enabling* conditions that accelerate development. The conditions are as follows:

The essentials:

Real team. The team is not a team in name only, but a bounded, stable and interdependent unit. Everyone is clear on who team members are. They remain together long enough as a team to learn to work together. They share accountability for a common purpose and have to work together to accomplish this.

Compelling purpose. The purpose for the team's existence is well specified, meaning that it is clear and that members know what success looks like. The purpose is also challenging, requiring a stretch to achieve it. The purpose is consequential, having a real impact on the lives and work of others.

Right people. Team members have the capacity to achieve the purpose, including the diversity, task and teamwork skills needed to work together effectively.

The enablers:

Sound structure. The basic structure for getting work done is clear and well designed. The team's work is motivating, the size of the team is just right and the rules of engagement (norms) are well specified.

Supportive context. Their systems enable and encourage teamwork. Team members are well rewarded and recognised for excellent *team* performance, rather than individual achievement. They have the information, training, time, money and resources they need to accomplish their purpose.

Team coaching. This is available to the team and provides real-time intervention to help the team make good use of its collective resources.

Wageman et al. define three criteria of team effectiveness:

1. *Task performance.* The output of the team (its product or services) meets or exceeds the standards of its clients or stakeholders.

2. *Quality of group process.* The social processes the team uses in carrying out the work enhance members' capability to work together effectively in the future.

3. *Member satisfaction.* The team experience contributes positively to the learning and wellbeing of individual team members.

The Six Conditions can be used as a conceptual framework with the team to aid discussion around what effectiveness means to them as a team. You can also use it as a checklist that the team can revisit periodically. You might also use the online assessment, Team Diagnostic Survey (TDS), to assess the team's effectiveness.

For more information, see **www.6teamconditions.com**

Authority Matrix

Ruth Wageman also introduced me to Hackman's (2002) Authority Matrix.

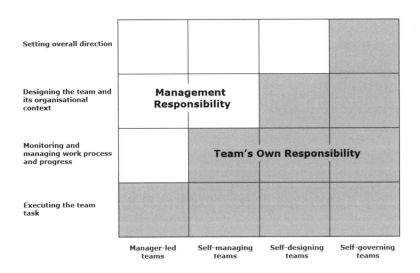

The Authority Matrix

Often missed by team coaches, but absolutely essential, is the work of identifying the authority structure that exists in a team. Hackman's model defines 'four levels of team self-management'. As you can see from the model, self-governing teams have authority over all four levels:

1. *Manager-led:* members have authority only for actually executing the task. Managers monitor and manage the team's work processes and progress.

2. *Self-managing:* members have responsibility not only for executing the task but also for monitoring and managing their own performance.

3. *Self-designing:* managers set the direction of the team. Members have authority for the design of the team and all other aspects of the work.

4. *Self-governing:* members have responsibility for all four of the major functions – deciding what gets done, structuring the team, managing performance and carrying out the work.

If this work isn't carried out explicitly, members will do it implicitly, running the risk of insufficient decision-making or overstepping the bounds of their authority.

What's more, in my experience of training and supervising team coaches, I find that many have not examined their own inherent leadership biases. This can result in the coach either unwittingly offering too many decisions to the team to make collectively, such as the team's vision and purpose, or the opposite, whereby the coach tries to push decision-making onto one leader in a team that is designed to be self-governing.

The Three Components

There are really only three broad categories that you can work with in team coaching; we call these the Three Components of Team Coaching.

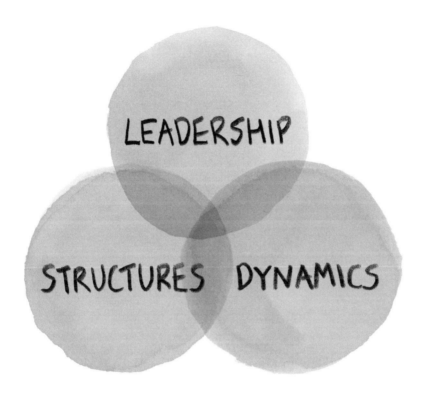

The Three Components of Team Coaching

Leadership: The ability to move from a directive style to one which is co-creative and, ultimately, towards the team's autonomous working. This will depend on the maturity level of the team and the demands of the specific situation at the time.

Structures: The frameworks, tools, exercises, processes and techniques that you might use in team coaching. Having a range of these available and understanding their suitability, effect and operation is important.

Dynamics: Understanding and being able to work with what is happening in the team and the team's system at the psychological level.

Waterline Model

The Waterline Model is based on Roger Harrison's article 'Choosing the Depth of Organizational Intervention' (1970). His aim was to provide a conceptual model which matches intervention strategies to particular organisational problems. The basic idea of the waterline model is simple. A team is always moving towards particular goals, and members are working on tasks to achieve them. When everything is working smoothly, it is deemed to be 'above the waterline'.

In reality, things rarely go smoothly, and the team will nearly always hit choppy water at some stage. At this point, we need to dive beneath the waterline, switching our focus from tasks to a focus on structure, process and people. This shift enables the team to understand what the obstacles are and to work out how to address them.

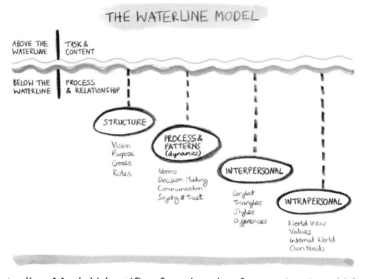

The Waterline Model identifies four levels of organisational life under the waterline where the source of the problems might be found: structure, process and patterns, interpersonal and intrapersonal. When problems occur, human tendency is to blame individuals, or to put issues down to personality differences or different styles of conflict. Many coaches love using tools to identify these. However, the majority of breakdowns occur in the first two levels in the Waterline Model. Maintenance starts at the surface; exploring possible causes of breakdown requires looking at each level and working your way down. Possible questions for exploring issues at each level are:

1. Structure
   - ➤ What are the goals?
   - ➤ What decision-making style are we using? Who has the decision-making authority?
   - ➤ Who's doing what, when?

2. Process and patterns (dynamics)
   - ➤ Is the team operating to clear and effective norms?
   - ➤ Is the decision-making process handled well?
   - ➤ Is communication effective?
   - ➤ How effectively does the team accomplish tasks?

3. Interpersonal
   - ➤ Do interactions get finished or interrupted?
   - ➤ Do members summarise and check for understanding?
   - ➤ Is conflict managed effectively?
   - ➤ Is feedback given and received effectively?
   - ➤ Do members learn from their experience?
   - ➤ Who is participating? Who is not?

4. Intrapersonal
   - ➤ Do I report my here-and-now experience? (Think, feel, want, sense, do.)
   - ➤ Do others report their here-and-now experiences?
   - ➤ Do I triangulate by speaking with others about issues I have with another team member, instead of talking with them directly?

The main principle is, when the team is stuck, to stop 'task' talk and to start 'maintenance' talk. Invite them to talk about what is happening at different levels under the surface, asking, 'What is happening in the team's processes that might be leading to this issue?' Before the team apportions blame or puts issues down to personality clashes, invite them to put on their goggles and dive below the waterline to understand where issues are inhibiting progress.

Cycle of Experience

Gestalt psychology has a significant influence on my work as a coach. It makes sense to me as a team coach especially, as it emphasises that the whole of anything is greater than the sum of its parts, and teams, by their very nature, are greater than the sum of each individual team member. *Gestalt* means a whole, pattern or form. Our lives are full of 'open gestalts', or unfinished business, such as projects started and not finished, conversations not meaningfully had, unresolved conflict and unfulfilled wishes. Throughout our lives, experiences emerge, take form, catalyse action and, when followed through, we experience resolution and satisfaction, and we close off the experience. Then a new idea forms and around we go again. In gestalt, this is called the 'cycle of experience'.

Imagine you are in bed, in a deep sleep. Through the movie of your dreaming, you hear a distant sound of a dog barking. You continue sleeping, and for a while the sound becomes a feature in your dream. The barking persists, and gradually you become aware of the insistent noise that had seemed like part of your dream. You start to wake, realising that your own dog is barking. For a moment, you lie still, wondering whether he'll stop. Eventually you decide you need to get up and see what he is barking at. You go downstairs and find him by the back door, urgently needing a pee. You let him out, he does his business and you put him back to bed. You climb the stairs and sink back into your own bed, hoping you can get back to sleep.

Cycle of experience

Another core concept in gestalt is that of *figure–ground*. In any situation, what we each pay attention to differs. Some things stand out – figure – and others remain in the background – ground. *Figures of interest* emerge from the ground, as illustrated in the cycle of experience above. The dog's bark emerged from the ground of your dreaming, until it became figure. Each figure draws our attention and is supported by an accompanying need.

For example, look at this picture below. Whether you see faces or vases depends on if you see the white as the figure or the black as the figure. If you see the black as the figure, then you see a vase. If you see the white as the figure, then you see two faces in profile.

Gestalt concept of figure and ground

When working with individuals, the coach guides the client in surfacing a meaningful figure of interest. This emerges from the 'ground' of the coaching conversation, gains momentum and catalyses action, ideally towards satisfactory resolution.

In teams, what is figure to one person (what stands out) in a meeting may be very different from what is figure for another. The significant challenge in team coaching, therefore, is how the team will generate a common figure of interest that is strong enough to keep the team's focus towards a meaningful outcome.

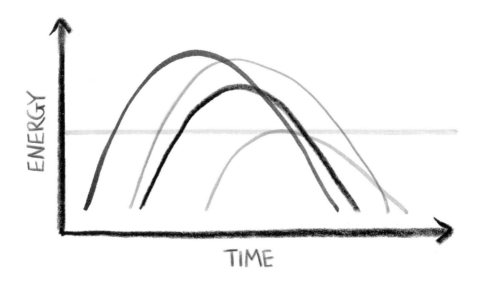

Multiple cycles of experience in team coaching

When team members are in different places on the cycle of experience, the team coach needs to slow down to speed up. Instead of pushing for agreement, they must work with the team to surface more of the ground, disclosing what they are thinking and feeling. Pushing for agreement gives the relief of having a common focus; however, with team member concerns driven underground, there is likely to be fairly low commitment to the conversation and any outcomes – the team is going through the motions.

The work here is about building the container, making it safer for members to disclose more. Then, by using the metaskills of presence and use of self, you help the team to increase their awareness of the multiple figures at play, which in turn leads to a more meaningful dialogue. For example, you might:

➤ keep inviting the team to gradually disclose more

➤ ask 'What do you notice is happening right now?'

➤ encourage team members to connect more with each other ('What do you hear Nishi say?' or 'What would you like to understand more of from Nishi?')

➤ use a mode 3 intervention, e.g. 'As I listen, I sense there may be a lot more to be said here; what else do you want to share?'

Eight Behaviours for Smarter Teams

Roger Schwarz (2013) describes eight behaviours that improve how team members work together. He provides more specific guidance on often used but relatively abstract statements like 'Treat everyone with respect'.

The Eight Behaviours for Smarter Teams
1. State views and ask genuine questions.

2. Share all relevant information.

3. Use specific examples and agree on what important words mean.

4. Explain reasoning and intent.

5. Focus on interests, not positions.

6. Test assumptions and inferences.

7. Jointly design next steps.

8. Discuss undiscussable issues.

Even though these behaviours are common sense, they can be hard to put into practice, especially when challenges occur and views differ.

By working explicitly with the eight behaviours, team members are able to apply them more consistently. When you introduce them to a team, explain how they can help the team to be more effective, giving specific examples. Also, invite team members to share their views, questions and concerns about the behaviours. Ultimately, it is important that people make an informed choice to adopt them, and it may be better to use an alternative set of behaviours than to impose these. Each of the behaviours helps the team in a different way so they work better as a complete set. However, it is better to use some of the behaviours than none at all.

For more on working agreements, visit the book website.

Team Charter

A team charter is effectively a form of contract, clarifying the outcomes the team is working towards and how they will work together. Coach the team to create their own charter and capture the results in a dashboard. Here is a sample team charter canvas:

TEAM CHARTER FOR (TEAM NAME) DATE:		
TEAM PURPOSE Why the team exists	**COMMON GOALS** What specific results do we want to achieve	**CORE VALUES** What do you care about?
MEMBERS Who is on the team?	**ROLES** What roles are necessary?	**KEY STAKEHOLDERS** Who are our key stakeholders and what do they need from us?
WORKING AGREEMENTS How do we commit to working together?	**DECISION MAKING** How will we make decisions?	**COMMUNICATION** How will we communicate with others?

You can find different examples of team charters in books and online. All too many charters get captured in a document and filed away on a server, never to be seen again. Creating a charter is only meaningful and worthwhile if it actually informs the team's focus and how they work together. It will therefore need referring to and updating frequently.

Checking In

Introducing a process of checking in is the simplest way to start building a container for your work as a team coach.

A check-in is a structure at the beginning of a team coaching session that includes everyone by giving each person the opportunity to speak in turn. While one person is speaking, everyone else listens to them.

The purpose of a check-in is to:

➤ help people to arrive (psychologically) and to become present and attentive

➤ get all the voices into the room

➤ help everyone to listen

➤ surface anything that might get in the way of people being present (such as your son being sick all night, or reversing your car into a tree)

➤ bring concerns and issues into the open so there are no unspoken thoughts or distractions from the session

➤ create energy and possibility

➤ initiate the direction of the conversation.

The real value of check-ins can be the sense of connection that happens when people speak their truth and speak from the heart. Therefore, encourage people to go beyond social-level content of their check-ins, such as the traffic or the weather, or what they cooked the night before. Invite them to go under the surface and to check in at psychological and emotional levels. It can take time for people to feel safe enough to check in at a deeper level, so accept some more superficial checking in to begin with.

There are various forms of check-in, and each has a different impact. Here are a few:

Variation 1: Talking stick

➤ Sit in a circle so everyone can see each other's face. Agree on the time you'd like to devote to the activity.

➤ Invite members to take two or three minutes to centre and ground themselves: 'Sit comfortably, in silence, breathing deeply and letting your eyes soften (or close if you prefer) while you become aware of the thoughts in your mind.' There are many creative ways of doing this, including music, mindfulness practice or simply taking a moment's silence to settle in.

➤ Invite anyone to start the process. The speaker may hold a talking stick, a stone or some other object that physically symbolises the 'right to speak'.

➤ The speaker takes some time to say whatever he or she wants, with no constraints. If the speaker does not want to speak, he or she can just say 'I pass', reserving the right to speak at the end of the circle or to not speak at all.

➤ While the speaker is holding the talking object, no one interrupts or responds to his or her statements. Someone may, however, choose to say something related to what has already been said, when it is their turn.

➤ When the speaker is done, he or she says, 'I'm in'.

➤ The speaker passes the talking object to the person on his or her left. The process is repeated until everyone has had a chance to speak.

Check-out

The check-out follows the same process. The only difference is that each person finishes by saying, 'I'm out.'

Variation 2: Ask a question

Ask a question that mines for emotions or issues that might not be spoken. Examples are:

➤ Describe your week in terms of the weather (e.g. stormy, cloudy, sunny, etc.)

➤ What was the highlight of this week, and why?

➤ What has been the most challenging aspect of work this week?

➤ If you were any animal, what would you be?

➤ If you could rid the world of one thing, what would it be?

➤ What's one thing you are excited about related to today's meeting? And something you're worried about?

Variation 3: Picture cards

1. Bring a selection of picture cards and spread them out on the floor so the images can all be seen.

2. Invite the team to walk around the picture collection and to select one that resonates with them right now.

3. Invite each person to speak about what the card means to them.

Variation 4: Jelly baby tree

1. Many versions of the jelly baby tree (sometimes called the 'blob tree') can be found online. Make sure you have a copy for each team member.

2. Invite team members to circle or colour in the figure they most identify with. They can draw on an additional figure if they like.

3. Then, one by one, invite them to share their chosen figure and why.

Four Player Model

David Kantor, a family therapist, started to observe how people were communicating in families. He realised that the same patterns were true in organisations. He noticed that in all interactions, there are only four possible speech acts:

A *move* is a suggestion, idea or course of action, such as 'Let's take a trip to the beach'.

A *follow* is supporting or agreeing with what has been said: 'That's a great idea.'

An *oppose*, which comes down to blocking, saying 'No, I don't fancy the beach – let's go to the mountains'.

A *by-stand*, either adding information or observing patterns: 'Dina hasn't said what she would like to do.'

Every one of these speech acts is important in a team. When someone makes a move, you get direction. When someone follows, you get support and action. When someone opposes, you get perspective. When someone by-stands, they raise awareness of what is happening in the group.

Teams become stuck when individuals overuse one of the four actions, again and again. When interactional patterns become habits, they can become entrenched, undermining group learning and effective decision-making.

The model is fantastic for identifying and modifying communication structures that take place 'in the room'. For more information see: www.kantorinstitute.com

Dialogue

From the Greek, the term 'dialogue' implies a 'flow of meaning'. The aim of dialogue is to surface ideas, perceptions and understanding that people do not already have. It is a shared inquiry, a way of thinking and reflecting together. This is unusual as people tend to enter conversations well prepared and with clear ideas. Distinctively, in dialogue, you explore uncertainties and questions that you don't already have answers to. Team dialogue enables them to think afresh together, beyond reporting old thoughts, enhancing their collective wisdom.

Kantor's Four Player model can give you valuable information about the effectiveness of team interactions. Dialogue invites a different kind of conversation, one that seeks to enrich and deepen the quality of the exchange.

Isaacs (1999) describes four behaviours for dialogue:

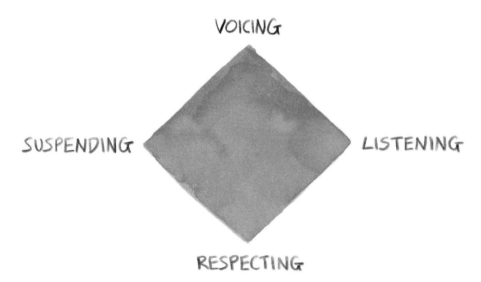

Four behaviours for Dialogue

Listening: We take listening for granted, but it is actually very hard to do. When we don't listen, all we have is our own interpretation. It is also important to listen together – voices and meaning are emerging from us all. Dialogue requires us to listen without resistance or imposition.

Respecting: Respect encourages people to look for sense in what others are saying and thinking. It requires awareness of the integrity of another's position and the impossibility of fully understanding it. Respect reassures and strengthens the genuineness in others. It enables you to challenge without evoking a negative reaction. True respect enables genuine inquiry.

Suspending: When listening to someone speak, we can resist their point of view – trying to get them to accept the 'right' way of seeing things. We can look for evidence to support our own view that they are wrong, and their thinking is flawed. This attitude creates 'serial monologues' rather than dialogue. By suspending our judgements, assumptions and opinions, we are suspending certainty too, releasing creative energy. This does not mean suppressing what we think; instead, we acknowledge and observe thoughts and feelings as they arise without feeling compelled to act on them.

Voicing: One of the most challenging aspects of dialogue, voicing is about revealing what is true for us, regardless of all the other influences that may be brought to bear. Voicing starts with listening internally, asking yourself 'What needs to be expressed now?' A team has a voice that wants to be articulated. Voicing is used to create a common pool of meaning together – speaking to the centre of a circle, with people speaking as a contribution to the whole.

Team Coaching Business Case

In his book *Coaching the Team at Work,* David Clutterbuck (2007) offers some useful questions for engaging the top management team in a dialogue in order to make a case for coaching a team:

➤ Is this organisation ready for team coaching?

➤ What are you relying on the team in question to do for the organisation?

➤ What are the consequences if it doesn't deliver?

➤ How would you know if it doesn't deliver?

➤ How much effort are you prepared to put in to make sure that it does deliver?

➤ What are the chances of it doing so without coaching?

➤ What has the payoff for team coaching got to be to cover the investment costs of time and imported coaching expertise?

➤ How would you measure the payoff?

➤ What are the risks, if any, of providing team coaching?

Team Coaching Readiness

In Chapter 4, we considered team coaching readiness through the lens of the Six Conditions for Team Effectiveness. Below is a checklist you can use to assess the team's readiness for coaching:

Team Coaching Readiness Assessment:
➤ Does the team see itself as 'a team'?
➤ If not, does it see value in becoming a team?
➤ Does the team have a clear and compelling purpose?
➤ Does the team have goals that require the collective effort of the team?
➤ Is the team membership likely to be relatively stable during the team coaching?
➤ Is the team the right size for the collective work?
➤ How on board and motivated is the leader for team coaching?
➤ How on board and motivated are team members to engage in team coaching?
➤ Is the team leadership effective enough for team coaching?
➤ Does the team recognise the need for change? Is the leader willing to be coached? If so, in private or with the team present?
➤ Are members prepared to work through issues openly?
➤ Is there a genuine desire for change?
➤ To what extent does the team understand the coaching process?
➤ To what degree is the team coaching sponsored from the leadership outside of the team?
➤ What involvement will the sponsor(s) have, and what are their expectations of the team coaching?
➤ Is the team able and committed to dedicate the time necessary for the team coaching?
➤ What obstacles might get in the way of the team coaching?
➤ How healthy is the team? Are there high degrees of dysfunction or toxicity?
➤ What reservations do the leader/members/sponsors have about team coaching?
➤ What reservations do you, the coach, have?
➤ Do you, the coach, have the resources you need to coach this team?

Self-generated Team Assessment

Here is a fantastic activity that you can use with a team to explore their experience of great teams, and to use their findings as a model and assessment of team effectiveness. It begins with inviting the team to share their best and worst team experiences and to identify key 'best team' attributes from their stories. Then they turn these into a model of team effectiveness, against which they can regularly assess themselves as a team.

Step 1

1. Invite team members to individually recall the best ever team they have experienced. This is ideally from a work context; otherwise, they can pick a sporting or other context out of work where there was a real spirit of teamwork. Ask them to spend a few moments remembering the team, running scenes like a movie through their mind. They should recall what the energy and atmosphere was like and remember how it felt.

2. Now ask them as a whole group (or in smaller groups if the team is large) to share their stories with each other. While doing this, they are to capture on a flipchart the attributes that made their remembered teams great.

3. Repeat steps 1 and 2 but with the worst team they have ever experienced. Allow time for storytelling as this supports them in recalling the significant impact a bad team can have on people's emotions and mood.

Step 2

1. Give the team 20 minutes to work together to identify the top eight attributes of 'best teams'. (Note: by limiting them to eight, the team will need to collaborate to decide on the final selection.)

2. Now ask them to write each attribute on individual sheets of paper and then to turn this into a Best Teams model.

3. Quietly observe this process in action (using modes 2 and 3) without trying to 'fix' any obvious dysfunction like one person dominating the conversation or others opting out.

Step 3

1. Invite the team now to step back and recall how they worked together during step 2 of the activity. Ask them to discuss this between themselves and to assess themselves against their own model.

2. Explore what were their strengths, what attributes were less applied and how these might inform potential development areas for the team.

Step 4

➤ Ask for permission to share your own observations to build on or confirm their self-assessment.

Note:

➤ You can use the resulting team attributes model as a guide for the team values, behaviours and working agreements.

➤ The team can periodically test themselves against this using their own model to see if they are being the best team they can be.

Empty Chair

Originating from gestalt and systemic approaches, 'empty chair' work gets the voice of stakeholders into the room, is remarkably simple and can be very powerful. An empty chair is nominated for the 'voice of the team'. Team members are invited to take turns to sit in this chair and respond to a topic or question from the team voice. This chair acts as a means for team members to think beyond their own voice.

Here's the process:

1. Invite the team to map out their stakeholders on a flipchart.
2. Elicit the top three to five 'primary stakeholders' (e.g. the executive, customers, suppliers, other teams, etc.).
3. Place an empty chair in the room.
4. Invite a team member who has the most resonance with the first stakeholder group to sit in the chair and to speak as that stakeholder (e.g. what it feels like to be them, how they see the team, what their needs are from the team, etc.).
5. Cycle until all stakeholders have been represented.
6. Debrief this as a team; invite the team to consider the stakeholders' needs in the purpose and ways of working.

Things to explore from the stakeholders' point of view could include:

➤ What matters most to your stakeholders (perhaps naming each stakeholder, or groups of stakeholders like 'the board', 'customers', 'staff', etc.)?
➤ What does success look like for your stakeholders?
➤ What do stakeholders expect of you as a team?
➤ What might your stakeholders' concerns be about the team?

Using pictures, drawings or objects

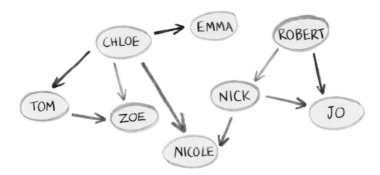

There is a well-known saying 'a picture is worth a thousand words'. Drawing can be used in so many ways in team coaching. Pictures can reveal so much information and they can often reveal what is held more at the emotional level, or what is not being said.

Here are some ways you can use drawing and/or pictures:

1. Invite team members to bring a picture (or object) from home that has significant personal meaning. Then, in the team session, invite them one by one to share the picture and speak about what it means to them.

2. Invite team members to individually create a picture of their 'dream team'. They can then share the elements of their picture before working together to create a picture of 'one dream team'.

3. Ask team members to create a 'relationship map' showing team members' relationships with one another. The closer the relationship, the shorter and bolder the lines between team members.

4. Offer up a collection of objects, such as peg dolls, Lego, counters or, depending on what is available in your setting, water bottles, drink mats or sticky notes. You can use identical objects or a variety (such as a range of Playmobil figurines). Invite team members to select several and to create a sculpture of the team using the objects. I suggest that you are unspecific as to what the objects mean, allowing team members to place their own meaning.

Sculpting

This is a technique that can be used to explore relationships, themes such as power and decision-making, or team alignment. While it is often taught as an in-depth technique, if used flexibly and loosely, it can be quick and effective. I find it most helpful for *creating awareness* around human dynamics. It can reach beyond cognitive meaning-making through words and language, inviting a more spatial and emotional experience into the work.

Here's a simple distillation of the process:

➤ Ask the team to find an object to represent 'something' and to place it in the middle of the room. The something will be a figure of interest, for example the team's purpose or vision, a decision, or even a word like 'trust' or 'connectedness'.

➤ Invite the team to move around, without discussion, and find a place to stand which symbolically represents their relationship with the 'something'.

➤ Invite each person to make a statement about what they are noticing or experiencing from their position.

You can then develop this, for example:

➤ Invite team members to move to a different position. Then explore what this move represents for them.

➤ Invite the team to collectively, and without discussion, make a move towards 'better'.

This technique is similar to 'systemic constellations', which are equally effective at *creating awareness* around dynamics and unspoken needs at play. John Whittington's excellent book *Systemic Coaching and Constellations* (2012) describes the principles and process in more detail.

Four Horsemen of the Apocalypse

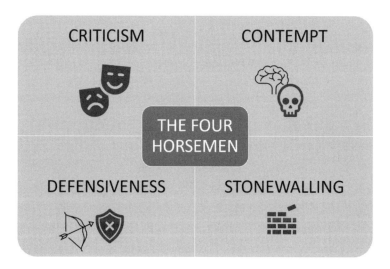

John Gottman of the Gottman Institute uses the four horsemen of the apocalypse as a metaphor to describe four communication styles that are deeply toxic to relationships. The work derives from couples counselling, and Gottman is said to be able to predict divorce with 90 per cent accuracy. As all relationships rely on communication, the findings are equally valuable in any form of relationship, including teams.

The four horsemen are:

➤ *Criticism* – verbally attacking someone's personality or character

➤ *Contempt* – attacking someone's sense of self with an intent to insult or abuse

➤ *Defensiveness* – victimising yourself to ward off a perceived attack and reversing the blame

➤ *Stonewalling* – withdrawing to avoid conflict and convey disapproval, distance and separation.

Help the team to understand the Four Horsemen and coach the team to discuss and agree behaviours to counter these toxic ones. You can read more about the four horsemen and their antidotes at **www.gottman.com/blog/the-four-horsemen-the-antidotes/**

Raising sensitive issues

One of the most common areas that team coaches bring to supervision is how to raise sensitive issues. The 'elephant in the room' is a phrase that describes the issues and dynamics that we know exist, but don't have the courage or ability to talk about. Such issues get in the way of performance and make teamwork miserable. Teams can be paralysed by secrets and unexpressed issues and resentments.

It is therefore critical that teams learn to address 'undiscussables' in a safe and honest way. When they are named with care, energy that is bound up in holding back from expressing these thoughts and feelings gets released.

Here is an approach for surfacing elephants in the room, creating genuine dialogue and finding a way forward.

Naming elephants

First, help to prepare the ground and build the container for the session by stressing that:

➤ all issues are shared and owned by the team, rather than attributed to one or two people

➤ commitment to a resolution must be shared, and owned by the team

➤ there will be no blame or scapegoating.

Materials: identical pens and three Post-it notes or index cards for each team member.

The process is as follows:

1. Introduce the exercise by sharing the steps to be taken.

2. Establish the ground rules above.

3. Give each team member three cards and ask them to write down the top three things the team needs to talk about and those it isn't (the undiscussables). Give two ground rules:

   ➤ write in capitals

   ➤ no individual can be named, and it is not an opportunity to criticise another team member.

4. Collect the cards and shuffle them.

5. Ask the team to work together to put the cards in a continuum from the most discussable to the least (ideally putting them on a wall). Ask them to group any themes.

6. Then ask them to pick the three most undiscussable.

7. Invite the team to discuss them one at a time. Let the team choose the running order.

8. Now hold the space as the group engages in dialogue:

   ➤ maintain the ground rules

   ➤ encourage exploration of the issue from different perspectives

   ➤ intervene using modes 2 and 3 to support the naming of patterns and emotions

> ➤ encourage the expression of feelings to release the bound-up energy

> ➤ gradually start to encourage exploration into possible solutions.

9. Invite team reflection on the process:

> ➤ Ask what benefits have come from the dialogue.

> ➤ Ask them to share with each other what they have learned.

> ➤ Coach team members to connect with each other (e.g. 'Imran, what do you value about what Adam has just shared?').

There are many ways you can vary this approach:

Variation 1

Invite team members to write one undiscussable on a piece of paper (in capitals) and then to fold and put them in a bowl. Everyone picks one folded paper from the bowl. One by one they read what is written on their paper as if it were theirs.

Variation 2

Before organising and prioritising the cards, ask the team to list the gains and losses of not addressing the issues, for themselves personally, as a team and for the organisation. This can help the team to become aware of how the undiscussables are weighing the team down.

The real skill here is not in the activity itself, it is in how you use your presence to hold the space and generate dialogue, with *use of self* interventions to surface issues and dynamics. Here are some key considerations:

➤ **Make sure you have done container building work with the team first. You will need to manage the safety in the room.**

➤ **Manage the boundaries, regulating blame, criticism or personal attacks by reminding the team of the ground rules.**

➤ **Emotions may be charged, and feelings will need to be aired before resolution can be found. You will need to hold the space really well.**

A final word on tools

The frameworks, tools and techniques that you bring to team coaching can add colour and variety to your work. There are so many possibilities that I could write a whole book on this alone.

Visit the website for this book to discover more frameworks, tools and techniques.

I encourage you to use tools and techniques with a light touch, otherwise you risk teaching the team that you will always bring concepts and exercises to fill the time and to answer the question 'What are we going to *do* in the session?' Teams can easily avoid taking responsibility and come to see team coaching as a form of play or team entertainment. And, as their coach, you may fall into the trap of enabling the team to avoid doing the more challenging yet transformative work of real team coaching.

Reflection time

As you have seen, there are numerous tools, methods, models and techniques for working in a range of ways with teams.

Think about your team coaching toolkit (we use the word 'tools' to include all of your frameworks, theories, exercises, activities and techniques, etc.). Ask yourself:

➤ What tools do you have already? Make a list. Sort the list into an order to keep all of your tools visible so they are ready to use when the need arises. For example, which tool(s) might you use to help a team discover its purpose; which for naming tricky dynamics, etc?

➤ Which tools have you used regularly and which not at all? Are you overusing some tools out of habit and underusing (or completely forgetting) others?

➤ Which tools do you need to discard to make way for alternative ones?

➤ Similarly, which tools are no longer congruent with your team coaching philosophy or stance that would benefit from being thrown out or adapted to fit better?

➤ What makes you and your approach as a team coach unique? Do your tools align with this? For example, if you say you are a solutions-focused team coach, do you use scaling (e.g. 'on a scale from 1–10, where 10 is high, how do you rate...', positive talk and 'the miracle question' (inviting the team to envisage and describe how the future will be different when the problem is no longer present) at least as a part of your approach?

➤ What tools do you know you are missing and would love to have in your toolkit? Add them.

What have you learned about the different conceptual frameworks, tools and techniques, and how will you integrate this learning into your team coaching approach?

13 The Road to Mastery

We don't receive wisdom; we must discover it for ourselves after a journey that no one can take for us or spare us.

– MARCEL PROUST

The 10,000 hours rule

What does it take to become a master in any given field? Malcolm Gladwell (2009) in his bestseller *Outliers: The Story of Success* says it takes 10,000 hours of practice.

In team coaching, it takes much more than this! The 'more' is not necessarily about hours; it requires a certain *quality* of practice. Think about brilliant violinists: they practise for hours, every single day. Look at incredible painters, like Matisse, Picasso or Turner. They created thousands of works, their artistry flourishing with each brush stroke. More than hours, the best way to get better at something is through intentional practice, which means practising in order to learn and improve. Intentional practice requires you to identify the edge of your competence. Learning and growth necessitates that you understand and play to your strengths – your comfort zone – and that you keep pushing yourself out of your comfort zone into uncharted water.

Intentional practice is ideal when you get into the arena to practise with peers and an experienced team coach, someone who can help you to see what you might not. They will offer you feedback on your skills and way of being. This feedback is priceless, as the purpose is helping you to improve.

Intentional practice requires an experimental attitude. This means noticing a gap or an opportunity in your practice as a team coach, and then deliberately experimenting from a mindset of 'I wonder how this might work'. Allard de Jong says in our courses, 'With this attitude you can swan dive or belly flop, as all mistakes are opportunities for learning.' If you are not getting out of your comfort zone and taking risks, then you probably won't experience many belly flops, but you are also confining your practice to be at the same level tomorrow as it is today.

The road to mastery is travelled by reflecting on your practice and becoming self-aware. Examine your own beliefs, judgements and assumptions and how they inform your meaning-making and choices.

You as team coach

Why do you want to be a team coach? Is it because you want to support teams in achieving greater performance? Perhaps you dream of enabling better collaboration in the world. Or maybe you want to foster organisational cultures based on communication, understanding and dialogue.

Now ask yourself the same question at a deeper, much more personal level. What lurks deep beneath the surface of the ocean of your hopes and dreams? Dive deep inside your own psyche: what lives there?

Most coaches are driven to work with teams for publicly held 'change the world' reasons, which are found in the answers to the first question. At the same time, we have a more private, often unconscious, need to heal ourselves. Your first team was your family of origin. How you experienced your family growing up has shaped who you are today. It determines the roles you choose to play in groups, how you relate to power and authority and how you get your own needs met.

Imagine you were a middle child, and spent many hours playing referee between warring siblings. This primed you in later life with outstanding skills in mediation and working with conflict. Less well developed is your capacity to look after your own needs, so you withdraw into your shell when upset or triggered. Issues from your family of origin, if not sufficiently processed and dealt with, will surface when working with teams. Reflecting on your family of origin will raise your awareness and help you to manage yourself and make choiceful interventions in the room.

> The problem with the unconscious is, it's unconscious.
>
> – CARL JUNG

Of course, there are exceptions to the rule, and some coaches have done a lot of work on themselves through coaching and therapy. However, generally speaking, we will often re-create the same patterns and behaviours in groups that have been established as templates in our early years. We navigate our role in groups into familiar comfort zones. We engage in the same dysfunctional patterns that have got us into trouble time and time again. We respond to people based on the image we project onto them, not how they really are. Our relational style and maladaptive patterns that are present in all other areas of our life will appear in teams too.

It is this inner game that we need to explore as team coaches. One training course after another teaches you tools and skills to apply when dealing with other humans. But, if you don't have an awareness of these underlying aspects of yourself – and if they are disowned – you will not only project them onto others, but you are also likely to find them backfiring on you. When you are unaware or unaccepting of your wounds, you can get hurt when painful experiences emerge and, like *Groundhog Day*, there is a re-enactment of an episode in your life that you thought was long past.

Groups can provide corrective emotional experiences, giving you the opportunity to experience them in a new light. However, the place for this work is not when you are working with a team. It is the deep and personal work that takes place in the safe and supportive context of group supervision and, on occasions, therapy. It is likely that you will still get triggered from time to time when working with teams; we all do. However, presence requires us to manage our emotions and to remain grounded and present, whatever is occurring.

To enable you to work effectively with others, it stands to reason that you need to work on yourself.

So, if you want to dial up team effectiveness, connectedness and collaboration, then go to work on yourself. What aspects of you do you try to hide? What in your history shaped these aspects of you? What are your fears around having these parts revealed? How do you think that people will respond to these parts of you?

Working on yourself will enable you to choose to show up differently, to respond differently and to relate differently. You can safely revisit unfinished business from the past and continue the story with greater satisfaction – to some degree at least. When previously you ran for the woods, hurtling out of sight from a torrid group experience, now you can resurface into the world, ready to meet the moment.

Helen is a survivor. She grew up in a family destroyed by alcoholism and drug addiction. Her mother hit the bottle when she was nine years old. After a vicious fight her father had walked out, never to return. He was dead in less than two years from a massive drug overdose. Helen was the eldest of four children, and in the months and years that followed gradually became a single 'parent' of four – her mother, twin brothers and a younger sister. In the mornings, while her mother lay in a drunken stupor, she got her siblings out of bed and ready for school. She made sure they all had clean uniforms and packed lunches. After school, she cleaned the house and made a rudimentary supper from meagre supplies. The school didn't notice, and the authorities were unaware of the situation. To Helen, it had become so normal that she didn't question her situation or the role she was forced to play.

Fast-forwarding this snapshot of Helen's early years, we see her leave school at 16 and get a job as an office 'girl Friday'. Used to working hard and being reliable and capable, she was quickly promoted. By 23 she was an office manager, and at 29 she became the youngest 'chief' officer in the history of the organisation. To continue her development, the business sponsored her to attend a 'leader as coach' programme at a local business school. She quickly fell in love with coaching and realised it was her vocation. She easily developed relationships with people, and she enjoyed listening and understanding their worlds. Most of all, she wanted to make a difference.

Eventually she left and set up her own small coaching business. Her reputation grew, and after a few years, she had a steady stream of coaching clients, which is where she met Diana, the managing director of a healthcare organisation. New to the organisation, she asked Helen to provide team coaching to her senior leadership team to support them in operating as one team, rather than the siloed business she had inherited. Their relationship got off to a good start, as Diana shared with Helen her hopes and ambitions for the organisation and also confessed to the 'imposter syndrome' she was experiencing in her new role. Her power and vulnerability were compelling, and Helen quickly found herself caring deeply about Diana and the organisation's mission.

The initial team coaching was well received, and the senior team made real progress in terms of working together on strategic goals. Diana was so pleased she spent more and more time with Helen, sharing her daily challenges and asking Helen's support and advice. When there were clashes in the team, she asked Helen to coach the warring pair. When urgent presentations were needed, she asked Helen to give her feedback, often resulting in Helen redoing the presentation from scratch.

By the time Helen had been working with Diana and the team for nearly a year, she was entrenched in every aspect of the business. She had declined new business and was working longer and longer hours for Diana, who started calling her early in the morning on her way to work, late at night and over weekends. The team relied on her when they were confused or stuck. Helen was quickly burning out. Somehow, she had managed to feel responsible for the team's performance and for all the organisational challenges.

Thankfully, Helen engaged a supervisor, where she came to realise that she needed to feel needed and to know that she was essential to the survival of her new 'work family'. Armed with this awareness, Helen was able to recontract with Diana and the organisation to step back from the role she had become embedded in. She also set about consciously creating a new work family, in the form of a small consortium of coaches who formed strong bonds and provided each other with community and support. Helen learned to manage her need to take charge and be overly responsible for everyone and everything. Her colleagues were aware of her script and helped her to regulate this aspect of herself.

As you can see, Helen's childhood had taught her that she was responsible for the very survival of her family and she had come to see that her role in life was to take care of everyone and everything. In transactional analysis terms, this had become her 'script', running like a computer operating system, determining her decisions and behaviour. Her outstanding capacity to be resourceful, even in the face of the most problematic situations, was a tremendous strength. However, her shadow side was her disowned need to be needed. Indeed, she almost felt like she didn't exist without being continually in demand to help others. Through supervision she realised that she was creating a form of co-dependency that was as much about her own needs as those of her client and, by their reliance on her, they were rejecting their own agency as a team to deal with situations by themselves.

Unfortunately, we coaches can pay more attention to the team and the tools we use than we do to ourselves. This is flawed thinking. We bring ways of looking at the world; stories that determine how we look at the world and act on the world we perceive.

I ask you to know so much about yourself that you can predict and understand and regulate your interventions. It's a huge requirement.

> This is a virtuous circle in that inner change alters outer behaviours. For example, as a person matures, deals with more of their shadow and unfinished situations, we generally see less defensiveness and volatility, the need to control and be right, or to offer uninvited opinions and advice.
>
> – PETER BLUCKERT (2019)

Vertical development

We all know that changing ourselves is extremely hard. Over the last few decades, organisations have run countless leadership development programmes, packed full of tools and techniques for how to be a better leader. At the end of each programme, participants commit to making big changes; yet within a few weeks, days or even a few hours, the old habits return. Why is this?

➤ We know what we should be doing, but we don't do it!

➤ We struggle to translate learning in the 'real world'.

➤ We spend too much time learning content and not enough time working on ourselves.

Team coaching mastery is more about your own development and less about learning content. It is more about hours of practice in the arena, and reflective practice outside of the arena, than around digesting a catalogue of tools and techniques. It is not an event; it is a journey of growth that takes place over time.

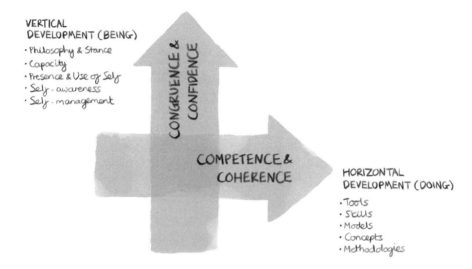

Vertical and horizontal development in team coaching

Nick Petrie's notion of *vertical development* (2014) beautifully encapsulates this and invites us to ask ourselves 'What if the problem isn't what you know, but who you are?'

A metaphor often used to describe *horizontal* development is a glass of water. The glass fills up as more 'water' – knowledge, skills, models – is poured in. People who are searching for new tools and techniques are looking to fill their glass. From this perspective, excellence is achieved by filling the glass with as much content as possible. Eventually, your glass gets full and you *know* it all. You just can't *be* it. The problem isn't the content, it's the glass. Successful team coaches pay more attention to the glass than the content. The glass is your philosophy and stance – the mindset and internal capacities you develop as a team coach. The aim is not to add more content to the glass but to grow the glass itself.

Horizontal development of learning tools and skills still matters. But the holy grail comes when these are integrated into who you are as a team coach – so horizontal and vertical at the same time. As you develop yourself, the way you think about and enact the team coaching competencies expands. Instead of filling your rucksack with a bunch of random tools and techniques thrown together, develop a coherent approach that coalesces around a set of guiding principles. Find your sweet spot in the Venn diagram of *who you are*, *what you think* and *how you work*.

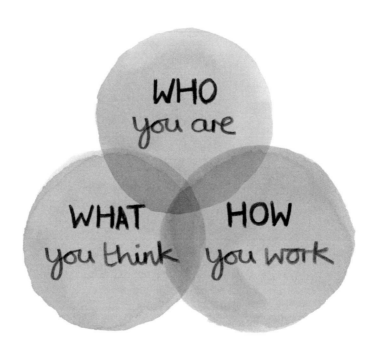

Mastery as a team coach requires that you engage in deep personal development, raising your awareness and consciousness. It requires you to flex your presence, contain the space, authentically self-manage and intervene intentionally, even in the most conflicted environments. The journey is one of ongoing integration of your practice into who you are as a team coach based on:

➤ your philosophy of change and human development

➤ how you see your role as a team coach

➤ a coherent methodology

➤ a style and presence that is congruent with how you talk about team coaching and how you show up.

Vertical development is inside out and involves a process that is based on reflection, raising awareness and generating insight. It requires a deeper self-examination that can lead to self-mastery as a team coach.

It is as much about unlearning as learning; it may involve letting go (of redundant beliefs and assumptions, hopes, judgements, personal biases, our narrative or something else). It can be a vulnerable experience, and it's not always easy, but it is liberating and deeply rewarding.

Intellectual understanding rarely transforms anything. Transformation happens when we free ourselves from the constraints of old experiences and stories which are impacting how we show up on a day-to-day basis. To develop range and presence as a team coach, we need to be energetically available and fluidly responsive to whatever is occurring in the present moment, and this requires the highest degree of self-awareness, courage and self-care.

Shuhari

Shuhari in kanji

Dr Krister Lowe hosted a brilliant podcast series called the Team Coaching Zone, in which he skilfully and sensitively interviewed team coaches from around the globe seeking to understand more about their practice. The coaches come from different geographies, schools and approaches, and the diversity of mind and style is truly inspiring. A couple of years ago, Krister introduced me to the Japanese martial arts concept of *Shuhari*. It describes the stages of learning from neophyte to master: *Shu* is about learning the 'form' from the master; in *Ha*, the student learns more deeply about the underlying principles and philosophy, and learns from others; in *Ri*, the student breaks free, creating their own approach, and adapts what they have learned to their own world view and circumstances.

This magical concept speaks powerfully to me. Learning team coaching begins with learning the 'form' – meaning the competencies, skills and etiquette defined by the profession – getting this into the bones of your practice. Then you explore more deeply into what informs the form and the ideas and beliefs that shape the skills. Also, widen your learning by seeking other teachers and schools, or by drawing from wider but related fields. Eventually, you will notice a new creativity, calling you to break free and to make your work your own. There are no shortcuts to mastery: it takes time and courage. You will have successes and failures along the way. Sometimes you'll want to give up. Find people in your life that will support you in keeping going – people who see the greatness in you.

Supervision in team coaching

> We are coaches precisely because we recognise that change is best supported through a relationship over time.

– THORNTON (2016)

> 'I am just not sure I can do this anymore,' I pleaded with my supervisor. 'I have started to dread going to team coaching sessions. I don't understand what is happening, but I end up feeling exhausted and counting time until I can go home.'

Some moments in team coaching have been the highlights of my career as a coach so far. Some have been the darkest moments, when I just wanted to crawl under my duvet and remain there for the rest of time. Team coaching can be exhilarating and deeply rewarding. It can also be draining and demoralising. If this resonates with you, you are far from alone. In his article 'Fear Factor', my colleague Declan Woods' (2014) research identified a prevalence of performance anxiety in team coaches which 'manifests itself either through internal doubts or in external concerns around value delivered for the team'. He goes on to say that 'even highly trained and experienced coaches became anxious when coaching teams, in a way that they don't while coaching individuals'.

This work can get under your skin, like no other. When you work as a team coach, you are inside the system, not standing outside of it behind some imaginary force field. When you are inside the system, it is impacting on you and you are impacting on it. If you are a member of the system that is to change, then you must be able to change and flex yourself. This is a challenging requirement. You need to know so much about yourself, to the depths of your being, as every aspect of you can make your way into the coaching space, and the coaching space can make its way into you.

As Woods says, 'This puts a premium on a coach's ability to recognise their own anxiety, be able to discern what is causing it, and either self-manage it to prevent it spreading to the team or use it productively for the service of the team.' Supervision can provide a safe and supportive space for reflection and dialogue. You look at your work from other perspectives in order to paint a richer picture of the system and its dynamics at play. Together, you explore the context and culture that the team is located with, examining the power and authority structures that pull and push what is possible. You dive into the relational dynamics, raising awareness of the impact the team is having on you, reducing anxiety and shame. Through the supervision process you find a fresh perspective, generate new ideas, and gain greater clarity and intentionality in your work. Most of all, you can regain your centre of gravity when anxiety destabilises you.

'I notice you seem very young and scared when you're talking,' said her supervisor. That was how Sandra felt. Like a child, scared to speak up and not knowing what to do. She was stuck in the mud of her emotions.

The team she was coaching was mired in conflict. She described one team member, Peter, who was particularly agitated, frequently sitting on the edge of his seat and tapping his pen loudly on the table. Sandra had opened up a conversation, asking what in their own experience contributed to a climate of trust. When it came to Peter's turn, he stood up and said, 'I don't trust anyone; it's not the way I am made. People need to earn trust.' Sandra asked him to share how people could earn his trust, to which he replied, 'They just need to know that I am right. I am always right!' He then got up and left the room, saying he needed the toilet.

Over the next two sessions, Peter's behaviour went downhill. Arriving an hour late, he then went to get coffee. He refused to answer any question that Sandra or anyone else asked, instead deflecting the question back to the team. When others spoke, he laughed or sneered and then piled in with criticism of their work, blaming them for various performance failures.

In supervision between sessions, Sandra and her supervisor explored the dynamics and rehearsed some responses. Now, with her third session looming, Sandra was feeling stuck, and her inner critic was telling her that she was a useless team coach. Through a gentle process of holding the space and exploration of her emotions, she was gradually able to rediscover her inner compass. The direction she chose to follow was to have a one-to-one with the team leader. She asked him to think back to when he hired Peter and what his understanding might be of his role. What emerged shed some light on the situation. New to the organisation, Dave had real concerns about the team's performance. On hiring Peter, he told him that his role was to be a 'disruptor', challenging the status quo and finding better ways of working. Peter was doing exactly that! He was challenging everything in sight, saying that he knew better. Sandra was then able to help Dave to see that Peter was executing to the brief he was given, and coached the leader on recontacting with him around his role.

Often carried out one to one, I believe group supervision is preferable for team coaches as the supervision group often mirrors different aspects of the team's system. This means that the supervisee benefits from the different perspectives that inform the meaning-making process and from the different ideas generated by the group. Ideally, your supervisor will be an experienced team coach him or herself. Team coaching is far more complex than one-to-one coaching, and a supervisor who has not personally experienced working with challenging organisational dynamics is likely to be less resourceful than one who has.

The pulls on a team coach

When a role is missing or not executed, there is a void. When the team needs this role to function, the void becomes a vacuum, which can draw the team coach in. Before you know it, you have unwittingly become the role holder.

We call this phenomenon the 'pull on a team coach'. Think of teams you have worked with: what roles have you taken on, often outside of conscious awareness? We ask participants in our team coaching training this question, and some typical answers are agenda organiser, administrator, fixer, rescuer, parent, mediator, accountability monitor, police officer and many more.

Notice the impact on you as you read the example below. What do you notice in your body? How do you feel?

> Having been made redundant for the third time in her career, Holly was increasingly despondent in her search for a new role. She was an experienced design director, but the market was flooded each year with bright young graduates with impressive portfolios, with twice Holly's energy and prepared to work for a third of her usual salary. She loved design, but she knew it was time to give up. She may as well get a job in the local supermarket for the time being. As her coach, you are feeling the weight of Holly's dejection. She looks up at you with tears running down her cheeks, and says, 'What shall I do?'

Do you sense a tightness in your chest, stomach or elsewhere? Do you feel protective of her, with a strong urge to help or even to fix her situation? Do you want to ask for her CV, saying you'll put it out to your network?

The 'pulls' happen frequently in any coaching relationship. We literally feel pulled into playing a specific role. In Holly's situation, perhaps you feel the need to rescue her. In the team situation, perhaps you are being pulled into the role of bringing order by playing traffic cop. These situations play out in large scale, like the team situation above. They also play out in micro-moments, as when a team member shivers, pulling a scarf around her while looking at you, appealing to you to close the window.

Teams are complex systems, and their dynamics are always swirling around under the surface to a greater or lesser degree. In team coaching, the feelings which team members are unable to express get displaced or transferred to you, the coach. For example, a team is getting increasingly frustrated as they struggle to agree on a business-critical decision. Do you feel their frustration and try to resolve it by facilitating them through a process of voting? Or do you recognise that pull that you feel to remedy the situation is actually the team as system revealing itself? It is creating awareness of the fact that the team do not have an effective process for making decisions when they don't all agree. Neither is right or wrong, it's simply a choice point for the coach, depending on the STS (self, team and situation).

The significance of the pulls on the team coach are that they are a powerful source of insight into unexpressed needs and the non-verbal ways that team members get them met. By becoming aware of the needs at different levels of the system – individual, team or organisational – you can be curious about them and invite the team to experiment with ways to get them met.

The longer you work with a team, the more you will be able to see patterns of emotions and interpersonal dynamics expressing themselves.

Developing as a team coach

As you near the end of this book, I hope that you have gained some insight and feel inspired to continue on your journey to becoming a more competent and successful team coach. That was my reason for writing it. But I am aware that the linear and sequential way of describing the process falls short of the lived experience. The reality is rarely an A to B trip; instead, it's an expedition rife with stops, restarts, diversions, U-turns and dead ends.

There is so much that I haven't had the space or found the words to say. I know I often find myself expressing things in talks, masterclasses and workshops that emerge from a deep vein of experience, good and bad. Perhaps, as a result of completing this book, I will find ways of identifying and articulating these missing components.

Certainly, you cannot learn team coaching by reading a book. Just as you can't learn to speak a language by reading about the language: you have to utter the words, practise the sounds and intonation, and get the language into your being so that, when they are required in conversation, the words just come to you without the need for a dictionary or phrase book.

Developing as a team coach is a process of learning through high quality training (on team *coaching*, as distinct from facilitation, team training, mentoring or consulting), ongoing reflection, supervision (by an experienced team coach), peer support and dialogue and, most of all, practice, practice, practice.

If you would like to find out more about our work at the Team Coaching Studio, including team coaching courses, supervision, community of practice, and the Team Coaching Arena (an online club where coaches get *into the arena* and hone their skills) then visit www.teamcoachingstudio.com or contact me at **georgina@ teamcoachingstudio.com**. I assure you of a warm welcome.

Georgina Woudstra

Reflection time

Let us start by saying that there is no such thing as perfect team coaching or the perfect team coach. This is a wholly unrealistic expectation and a pathway to much anxiety and misery as it is an unobtainable goal. That isn't to say we can't strive to become masters of the craft of team coaching. Start by seeking to master yourself.

Self-mastery starts with 'knowing thyself' according to the ancient Greek aphorism. Consider:

➤ personal reflection and reflexivity

➤ supervision (with a focus on self as team coach), preferably with a supervisor with experience of coaching teams

➤ therapy, either individual or group, which also gives you experience of being a group member

➤ gaining feedback from others, including co-/paired team coaches and teams we work with.

Give yourself the chance to do your best work. Start by looking after yourself. If you don't, it is unlikely you will be able to look after teams very well. Self-care can take many forms including:

➤ basics like ensuring we have enough sleep, rest, holiday, food, etc.

➤ turning off (or at least down) our inner critic and negative self-talk

➤ re-framing 'bad' team coaching as an opportunity to learn, including taking the positives from an experience as well as learning from things that may have gone less well.

The quality of your practice is more important than the quantity. Ask yourself:

➤ What do I want to practise in this team coaching session? What do I want to start/stop/continue to do or do more/less of this time? Focus as much on the 'being' of a team coach as the 'doing' aspects.

➤ Who can provide me with feedback on my team coaching and how? Can you record it (with permission) to replay and learn from later?

➤ Reflect after the team coaching: what worked well with my team coaching? Where might I be even better next time? What is my development goal next time I team coach?

➤ Shift from reflecting after team coaching to reflecting in action – during it. Try to develop your capacity to do this and notice the difference this makes.

➤ How can I increase the opportunities to practise team coaching? Ask a team! It doesn't have to be a long or formal engagement. You might strike a reciprocal agreement to provide some pro bono team coaching for some feedback and a reference and/or case study.

➤ As well as increasing the amount of your team coaching experience, try too to increase the variety of teams you work with. This should increase your ability to work with different types of team and presenting issues, and help you find out with what teams you do your best work.

➤ Ask 'With what types of teams, on what types of topics, and in what ways have I coached?' What did you learn from this exploration? What are the conditions for you to do your best team coaching? How do you put these in place (e.g. contracting with teams; turning down opportunities that are not the best fit for you, etc.)

Intentional practice is far more valuable than unguided practice. Determine your intention by asking:

➤ Where are your strengths as a team coach that you can develop further and excel at? What are key gaps to fill? In which areas are you less happy with your team coaching practice? Decide your learning edge.

➤ What's within and outside your comfort zone?

➤ What scaffolding (support) do you need to move from your comfort to your stretch zone?

➤ What have you learned about mastering the art of team coaching, and how will you integrate this learning into your team coaching approach?

GLOSSARY

The arena   When referred to in this book, I am talking about practising actual team coaching through role play or working with a real team, inspired by Brené Brown's (2012) work on vulnerability and shame. Real team coaching takes the courage to be vulnerable.

Armour   I use this term to define the psychological and emotional defence mechanisms we use to 'protect' ourselves and avoid showing who we really are and how we are being impacted. For example, maybe you are afraid of being judged so you portray an image you think others will expect from you.

Check-in   To engage in team coaching and dialogue, we need to be present. People arrive to team coaching 'carrying their baggage' from their outside worlds, and this can distract them from being present. Checking in enables team members to become more present. Another function is that it gets everyone's voice into the room at the beginning. People are more present once they have spoken. It also helps team members to connect with each other more as human beings. A third aspect of a check-in is to surface anything that might be in the implicit field that may impede the session if it is not shared.

Chemistry session	A standard practice in one-to-one coaching, a chemistry session is a preliminary meeting where coach and client discuss the aims of the coaching and establish 'fit' and whether they can work together.
Container	This is the 'psychological space' in which coaching takes place. It is the coach's role to help the team to co-create the space in which knowledge, understanding, learning, energy, ideas, tensions and dissonance can be contained. Over time, the coach transitions this role to the team itself, which then maintains its own container.
Content and process	*Content* refers to our thoughts and words. As a coach, it is often easy to get drawn into floating along with these. *Process* refers to how the client (team) goes about their business, including patterns of interaction and behaviour. The primary reason for mis-understandings and tensions is often less to do with the content and more to do with the process.
Countertransference	I am using this in the contemporary relational sense, meaning the coach's feelings and attitude in response to the client's (individual or team) transferences. Together, transference (*see below*) and coun-tertransference create a continuous cycle of mutual reciprocal influence.
Felt sense	Gendlin (2003) describes the felt sense as an *inner knowing* or 'a special kind of internal bodily awareness... a body-sense of meaning'. Although it has an emotional aspect, it is often somatic and is evoked in the coach in the presence of the team.

Field/field theory	A 'world view' (*see below*) that sees reality as holistic and interrelated. Everything occurs in some context. A fish in water means something different to a fish on a plate. The meaning of any situation is determined by the relationship between what we are focusing on (figure) and the context (ground) (*see below*). So, behaviour is a function of a person in an environment.
Figure–ground	A gestalt psychology principle which states that people instinctively perceive objects as either being in the foreground or the background. They either stand out prominently in the front (the figure) or recede to the back (the ground).
Figure of interest	Figures emerge and become the objects of our interests. The figures that emerge are influenced by human needs..
Frame of reference	*See 'World view'*
Gestalt	A psychological approach used in therapy, coaching and organisational development. At its heart is the co-created client–practitioner relationship as a method for exploring and increasing awareness, inviting experimentation and greater choice. This heightened awareness can help individuals and teams to find new perspectives, and new ways of being and interacting.
Groupthink	A psychological phenomenon where group members set aside their own beliefs and adopt the opinion or the choices of the rest of the group in the desire for harmony or conformity.

Here-and-now	Working in the here-and-now means staying grounded in the real experience that is unfolding in every moment in coaching, such as the actual words used, body language, the mood, energy, emotion and intentional patterns. By focusing on what is being played out in the here-and-now, clients can experiment with and embed changes which can be taken forward into everyday life.
Holding the space	This is the process of containing the tensions and intensities that arise without reacting to them. Typically, when faced with conflict, people have a tendency to align with the person they feel is 'right'. This limits the space in which new understandings can emerge, so 'holding the space' means suspending assumptions and demonstrating respect for all perspectives. Maintaining boundaries is also an essential component of holding, so that people know they are in a safe pair of hands.
Parallel process	A phenomenon occurring between coach and supervisor whereby the client's experiences or dynamics are re-created in the supervisory relationship.
Projection	An unconscious process where we attribute disowned parts of ourselves to others. These parts are often characteristics that we do not like and prefer to not be aware of. For example: I don't like to think of myself as arrogant, so I project (regard) another person as arrogant.
Silos	According to Lencioni (2006), silos are 'the invisible barriers that separate work teams, departments and divisions, causing people who are supposed to be on the same team to work against one another'.

Sitting in the fire	This is about the coach's capacity to hold and contain a space which is intense. Metaphorically it may be 'too hot to handle'. It involves active self-management on the part of the coach to meet moments that arise with an open heart and mind, without giving them power. Instead, you breathe, ground yourself, notice and let the moments provide insight, and then let them go.
Soft eyes	Coined by the Gestalt International Study Centre, 'soft eyes' means hearing and seeing what is happening, rather than actively looking for something. It involves the ability to focus on the team's interactional process, rather than on individuals or on the content.
Supervision	Coaching supervision is a collaborative learning practice to continually build the capacity of the coach through reflective dialogue for the benefit of both coaches and clients. (See https://coachingfederation.org/coaching-supervision)
Taylorism	Frederick Taylor started the scientific management movement in the early 1900s, sometimes referred to as the 'man as machine movement'. He proposed that by driving efficiency through optimising and simplifying jobs, productivity would increase. Taylorism is in opposition to teamwork, which sees collaboration and collective intelligence as drivers of productivity.
Teaming	A term coined by Amy Edmondson (2010) meaning actively building and developing teams while a project is in process, in recognition of the fact that the team's composition may change at any time. 'Teaming is a verb. It is a dynamic activity, not a bounded, static entity.'

Transference	In this book, I am using the contemporary *relational* use of the term, meaning that the client (individual or team) relates to the coach (or another team member) in ways that help the coach understand what is needed. (*See also Countertransference.*)
Triangulation	Originating in family therapy, triangulation is most closely associated with the work of Murray Bowen (1985). He stated that any relationship system with two or more people is unstable and that, under stress, it forms itself into a system or triangle. The 'third' person is often used as a substitute for direct communication or as a messenger to deliver missives to the main party.
World view	A person's world view is their philosophy of life and the way they see and understand the world.

BIBLIOGRAPHY

Asay, T., & Lambert, M. (1999). The empirical case for the common factors in therapy: quantitative findings. In M. Hubble, B. Duncan, & S. Miller (Eds.), *The Heart and Soul of Change: What Works in Therapy.* Washington: American Psychological Association.

Berne, E. (1963). *The Structure and Dynamics of Organizations and Groups.* New York: Grove Press, Inc.

Berne, E. (1964). *Games People Play: The Psychology of Human Relationships* (1st ed.). New York: Grove Press.

Bluckert, P. (2015). *Gestalt Coaching.* Maidenhead: Open University Press, McGraw-Hill Education.

Bluckert, P. (2019). *A comprehensive guide to vertical development.* Peter Bluckert.

Brown, B. (2012). *Daring Greatly: How the Courage to Be Vulnerable Transforms the Way We Live, Love, Parent, and Lead.* New York: Penguin Randon House.

Clutterbuck, D. (2007). *Coaching the Team at Work.* London: Nicholas Brealy International.

Collins, J., & Porras, J. (1994). *Built To Last: Successful Habits of Visionary Companies.* Harper Collins.

Critchley, B. (2010). Relational Coaching: Taking the High Road. *Journal of Management Development*, 29(10), 851-863.

de Haan, E. (2008). *Relational Coaching.* Chichester: John Wiley & Sons Ltd.

de Jong, A. (2006). Coaching Ethics: Integrity in the moment of choice. In J. Passmore, & J. Passmore (Ed.), *Excellence in Coaching.* London: Kogan Page.

de Jong, A. (2020, December). *Team Coaching in a Virtual World.* Retrieved from www.MasteringTheArtOfTeamCoaching.com

Denham-Vaughan, S. &. (2013). SOS: a relational orientation towards social inclusion. *Menatl Health & Inclusion*, 17(2), 100-107.

Edmondson, A. (1999). Psychological Safety and Learning Behavior in Work Teams. *Administrative Science Quarterly*, 44(2), 350-383.

Edmondson, A. (2010). *Teaming.* San Francisco: Jossey Bass.

Gallwey, W. T. (2000). *The Inner Game of Work.* Toronto: Random House.

Gardner, H. (1984). *Frames of mind: The theory of multiple intelligences.* Basic BBooks.

Gendlin, E. (2003). *Focusing: How To Gain Direct Access To Your Body's Knowledge.* London: Random House.

Gersick, C. J. (1988). Time and transition in work teams: Toward a new model of group development. *The Academy of Management Journal*, 31(1), 9-41.

Gladwell, M. (2009). *Outliers: The Story of Success.* London: Penguin Books.

Gregersen, H. (2018, March-April). Better Brainstorming: Focus on questions, not answers, for breakthrough insights. *Harvard Business Review*, 64-71. Retrieved from *Harvard Business Review*.

Gregersen, H. (2018). *Questions Are the Answer: A Breakthrough Approach to Your Most Vexing Problems at Work and in Life.* New York: Harper Collins Publishers.

Hackman, R. (2002). *Leading Teams: Setting the Stage for Great Performances.* Boston: Harvard Business School Publishing.

Harrison, R. (1970). Choosing the Depth of Organizational Intervention. *The Journal of Applied Behavioral Science*, 181-202.

Hawkins, P. (2011). *Leadership Team Coaching: Developing Collective Transformational Leaders.* London: Kogan Page.

Hogan, C. (2002). *Understanding Facilitation: Theory & Principles.* London: Kogan Page.

Isaacs, W. (1999). *Dialogue and the Art of Thinking Together.* New York: Doubleday.

Karpman, S. B. (1968). Fairy tales and script drama analysis. *Transactional Analysis Bulletin*, 26(7), 39-43.

Katzenbach, J., & Smith, D. (1993b, 1999). *The Wisdom of Teams: Creating the high-performance organization.* Harvard: Harvard Business School Press.

Kegan, R. (1983). *Evolving Self: Problem and Process in Human Development.* Harvard University Press.

Kets De Vries, M. F. (2018, June 13). *Once You Have It All, What's Next?* Retrieved from Knowledge: https://knowledge.insead.edu/blog/insead-blog/once-you-have-it-all-whats-next-9356

Lawrence, P. (2019, June- December). *The Systems Coach (parts 1 to 4).* Retrieved from Centre for Coaching in Organisations: https://www.ccorgs.com.au/thought-leadership/white-papers/

Lencioni, P. (2006). *Silos, Politics and Turf Wars: A Leadership Fable About Destroying the Barriers That Turn Colleagues Into Competitors.* San Francisco: Jossey-Bass.

McGill, B. (2012). *Voice of Reason.* Sarasota: Paper Lyon Publishing.

Meadows, D. (2008). *Thinking in Systems.* Chelsea Green Publishing Company.

Meier, D. (2005). *Team Coaching with the Solution Circle: A Practical Guide to Solutions Focused Team Development.* Cheltenham: Solutions Books.

Mindell, A. (1995). *Metaskills: The Spiritual Art of Therapy.* New Falcon Publications.

Nevis, E. (1992). Gestalt Therapy and Organizational Development: A Historical Perspective, 1930-1996. *Gestalt Review*, 1(2), 110-130.

Nevis, E. C. (1987). *Organizational consulting: A Gestalt approach.* New York: Gardner Press.

Oshry, B. (2007). *Seeing Systems: Unlocking the Mysteries of Organizational Life.* Berrett-Koehler Publishers.

Petrie, N. (2014). *Vertical leadership development: Part 1: Developing Leaders for a complex world.* Retrieved from http://insights.ccl.org/articles/white-paper/

vertical-leadership-developmentpart-1-developing-leaders-for-a-complex-world/

Robson, M., & Beary, C. (1995). *Facilitating.* Aldershot: Gower Publishing Ltd.

Scharmer, C. O. (2018). *The Essentials of Theory U: Core Principles and Applications.* Oakland: Berrett-Koehler Publications, Inc.

Schein, E. (2013). *Humble Inquiry: The Gentle Art of Asking Instead of Telling.* San Francisco: Berrett-Koehler Publishers, Inc.

Schwarz, R. (2013). *Smart Leaders, Smarter Teams: How You and Your Team Get Unstuck to Get Results.* San Francisco: Jossey-Bass.

Senge, P. (2006). *The Fifth Discipline: The art and practice of the learning organization: Second Edition.* London: Random House.

Senge, P. M. (1999). *Dialogue and the Art of Thinking Toegther.* New York: Doubleday.

Siminovitch, D. (2008). The Power of Presence and Intentional Use of Self: Coaching for Awareness, Choice and Change. *The International Journal of Coaching in Organizations.*

Siminovitch, D. (2017). *Gestalt Coaching Primer.* Gestalt Coaching Works, LLC.

Stewart, M. K. (2019, June 18). *Why Psychological Safety is More Important than Trust.* Retrieved from The Modern Manager: https://www.mamieks.com/post/why-psychological-safety-is-more-important-than-trust

Thornton, C. (2016). *Group and Team Coaching: The secret life of groups.* Abingdon: Routledge.

Tuckman, B. (1965). *Psychological Bulletin*, 384-399.

Wageman, R., Nunes, D. A., Burruss, J., & Hackman, R. (2008). *Senior Leadership Teams: What It Takes to Make Them Great.* Boston: Harvard Business Review Press.

Wheatley, M. J. (2006). *Leadership and the New Science: Discovering Order in a Chaotic World.* San Francisco: Berrett-Koehler Publishers, Inc.

Whitmore, J. (1992). *Coaching for Performance.* UK/London: Nicholas Brealey Publishing.

Whittington, J. (2012). *Systemic Coaching and Constellations.* London: Kogan Page.

Woods, D. (2011). Coaches use of Reflective Journals for Learning. In J. (. Passmore, *Supervision in Coaching: Supervision, Ethics and Continuous Professional Development* . London: Kogan Page Ltd.

Woods, D. (2014, Sept/Oct). Fear Factor, in *Coaching at Work.*